Cambridge E

Elements in the Politics c
edited by
Rachel Beatty F
Einaudi Center for International Studies and Cornell University
Ben Ross Schneider
Massachusetts Institute of Technology
Maya Tudor
Oxford University

Mario Einaudi
CENTER FOR
INTERNATIONAL STUDIES

 MIT CENTER FOR INTERNATIONAL STUDIES

SHOCKS AND POLITICS

Understanding Disaster Preparedness

Jennifer Bussell
University of California, Berkeley

 CAMBRIDGE
UNIVERSITY PRESS

CAMBRIDGE
UNIVERSITY PRESS

Shaftesbury Road, Cambridge CB2 8EA, United Kingdom

One Liberty Plaza, 20th Floor, New York, NY 10006, USA

477 Williamstown Road, Port Melbourne, VIC 3207, Australia

314–321, 3rd Floor, Plot 3, Splendor Forum, Jasola District Centre,
New Delhi – 110025, India

103 Penang Road, #05–06/07, Visioncrest Commercial, Singapore 238467

Cambridge University Press is part of Cambridge University Press & Assessment,
a department of the University of Cambridge.

We share the University's mission to contribute to society through the pursuit of
education, learning and research at the highest international levels of excellence.

www.cambridge.org
Information on this title: www.cambridge.org/9781009635288

DOI: 10.1017/9781009635325

© Jennifer Bussell 2025

This publication is in copyright. Subject to statutory exception and to the provisions
of relevant collective licensing agreements, no reproduction of any part may take
place without the written permission of Cambridge University Press & Assessment.

When citing this work, please include a reference to the DOI 10.1017/9781009635325

First published 2025

A catalogue record for this publication is available from the British Library

ISBN 978-1-009-63528-8 Hardback
ISBN 978-1-009-63531-8 Paperback
ISSN 2515-1584 (online)
ISSN 2515-1576 (print)

Additional resources for this publication at: www.cambridge.org/Bussell

Cambridge University Press & Assessment has no responsibility for the persistence
or accuracy of URLs for external or third-party internet websites referred to in this
publication and does not guarantee that any content on such websites is, or will
remain, accurate or appropriate.

Shocks and Politics

Understanding Disaster Preparedness

Elements in the Politics of Development

DOI: 10.1017/9781009635325
First published online: February 2025

Jennifer Bussell
University of California, Berkeley

Author for correspondence: Jennifer Bussell, jbussell@berkeley.edu

Abstract: When will government elites prepare for natural hazards? Existing research posits that governments will respond to disasters, but rarely have incentives to prepare for them. This Element argues that disaster preparedness can, and does, occur in the context of both motivated ruling elites and a capable state. Ruling elites can be mobilized to lead preparedness efforts when there is a risk that past exposure to hazards will lead to political instability in the face of a future hazard. Where elites anticipate a threat to their rule in the face of a future hazard, due to substantial past exposure and significant opposition strength, they will be motivated to engage in disaster preparedness. The quality and character of these efforts subsequently depend on the government's capacity to coordinate the design and implementation of preparedness plans. The Element tests this argument using a medium-N, country case study approach, drawing on evidence from ten countries in Africa and three in South Asia, as well as subnational analysis in India.

Keywords: Disasters, preparedness, capacity, India, Africa

© Jennifer Bussell 2025

ISBNs: 9781009635288 (HB), 9781009635318 (PB), 9781009635325 (OC)
ISSNs: 2515-1584 (online), 2515-1576 (print)

Contents

1 Introduction

The eve of our first day of interviews in Maputo, Mozambique, the rain began. It poured down throughout the night and into the morning. At breakfast, others around us mentioned the potential threat of an incoming cyclone. Given that we were in town to talk with government and civil society actors about disaster preparedness, it seemed only appropriate that we press on with our plans for the day. Our hotel was a short ferry ride from downtown, but the road to the port was flooded. Thanks to the availability of a 4×4, we made it to the ferry station and then to the mainland. On arrival, we saw that the streets of Maputo, too, were awash in rainwater and debris, the sewer drains clogged by uncollected trash. On its face, the city was woefully unprepared for the ongoing storm.

But these issues masked what we later learned was happening in the background: active mobilization of government officials and nongovernmental actors to track the storm, prepare for any necessary evacuations, and activate additional precautions along the shoreline. Inland areas were pre-stocked with survival gear, such as boats, to be ready in the event of extreme flooding. While these preparedness programs were difficult for us as outsiders to observe, we nonetheless came to understand the significant ways in which the government in Mozambique had shifted the dynamics of cyclone threats to fundamentally improve the safety of at-risk populations. While these efforts might not ease immediate, less threatening, difficulties in the face of extreme weather (e.g. local, short-term flooding), they targeted high-risk issues that posed the greatest threats. To our good fortune, this tropical storm was not a particularly bad one, and the waters began to dissipate within a few days. Nonetheless, the experience offered a brief glimpse into the complex realities and practical difficulties associated with managing natural hazards.

This anecdote is also indicative of natural hazard experiences in many other parts of the world. As I came to understand during the research described in greater detail in this volume, significant preparedness efforts for natural hazards – such as floods, drought, and tropical storms[1] – have been taken on in countries around the world, including across the Global South. Governments, on their own and encouraged by global accords, have often implemented substantial programs that ensure both rapid response at the time of a hazard and work to minimize the risk that hazards evolve into natural disasters. In India, for example, a case I consider in detail throughout this text, government efforts to ramp up preparedness programs began to emerge in the early 2000s and a robust, multilevel system for threat identification, preparedness, and

---

[1] Tropical storm is a general term for cyclones, hurricanes, and typhoons, each of which is used depending on where the storm originates.

response now exists for multiple types of hazards. This is easiest to observe in cases where hazards in recent years have led to significantly fewer deaths than those resulting from previous similar events, as has been the case with recent cyclones in India.[2]

At the same time, the quality and comprehensiveness of these efforts can vary quite dramatically both across and within countries. In Mozambique's neighbor, Zimbabwe, we see relatively fewer efforts to prepare for frequent threats such as drought. Similarly, adjacent to India in Pakistan we observe relatively disorganized efforts to prepare for increasingly common flood risks. Even within India, at the state level, we note variations in the degree to which neighboring states such as Odisha and Andhra Pradesh are prepared for the threat of annual cyclones.

That disaster preparedness initiatives of any type appear in these regions is also a surprise from the perspective of existing research on political incentives and natural hazards.[3] A predominant assumption in current work is that investments in preparedness are fundamentally unlikely. This is because preparedness actions are expected to be more difficult to observe, and thus reward at the ballot box, than investments in response (Healy and Malhotra 2009). Analysts argue that citizens reward effective political responses to natural disasters and punish failures to respond (Healy and Malhotra 2009; Bechtel and Hainmueller 2011; Cole et al. 2012). At the same time, voters can fail to reward disaster preparedness, and may even punish incumbents for investing in preparedness over other public benefits, because the benefits of these policies are perceived to be less obvious that those of response (Healy and Malhotra 2009). This is despite the generally greater efficiency of spending on preparedness versus response (Healy and Malhotra 2009). In addition, the potential for moral hazard related to natural hazards, given the propensity of higher level domestic or international actors to respond in times of disasters, is believed to further disincentivize governments to allocate scarce resources toward preparedness activities (Cohen and Werker 2008). In short, existing work posits that political elites should have few incentives to prepare for natural hazards. Thus, the existence of, and variation in, disaster preparedness initiatives, even in closely lying countries or states facing similar hazards, is an empirical puzzle.

The primary focus of this Element is to examine this puzzle and provide a novel argument to explain the character of disaster preparedness initiatives in countries of the Global South. Why do governments prepare for natural

---

[2] See, inter alia, The Hindu, 2022.

[3] I focus here on literature pertaining to policy responses, but there exists substantial important and related work on factors affecting the quality of response (e.g. Aldrich 2010, 2012) and the downstream effects of natural hazards (e.g. Bhavnani and Lacina 2015).

hazards? And what characteristics of states are associated with the best preparedness outcomes?

I argue that disaster preparedness can, and does, occur in the context of both *motivated* ruling elites and a *capable* state. Ruling elites can be mobilized to lead preparedness efforts. The quality and character of these efforts subsequently depend on the government's capacity to coordinate the design and implementation of preparedness plans. In this way, elite motivation and state capacity are both necessary conditions that, when they occur together, are sufficient to produce comprehensive disaster preparedness. Thus, ruling elites must be *willing* and the state they oversee *able*.[4] My argument elaborates the conditions under which this occurs.

I contend, in contrast with existing work that argues politicians do not have incentives to prepare for disasters,[5] that there are plausible political situations in which ruling elites will perceive benefits to investing in preparedness. Specifically, elites are motivated when there is a risk that past exposure to hazards will lead to political instability in the face of a future hazard. Elite motivation thus rests on two sub-variables: past exposure to natural hazards and elite perceptions of opposition threat.[6] Where elites anticipate a threat to their rule in the face of a future hazard, due to substantial past exposure and significant opposition strength, they will be motivated to engage in disaster preparedness.

The ability of elites to act on this motivation depends on a second primary variable: the state's own competence in coordinating the bureaucracy and/or civil society actors to realize preparedness goals. Where government actors have the capacity to oversee preparedness efforts and are given the power to do so, ruling elites will plausibly succeed in implementing the highest levels of effective disaster preparedness.

In the remainder of this Introduction, I lay out a conceptual framework for analyzing natural hazards and disaster preparedness in the context of low- to middle-income countries of the Global South. I consider the relevance of this problem in the context of past threats in the region and across the globe more generally. I then elaborate the details of my argument for when governments are most likely to make preparedness investments, contrasting this with existing arguments for why governments would not invest in preparedness for natural hazards and the limited hypothetical conditions under which they would do so.

---

[4] This argument is consistent with the idea that state capacity matters most in the context of motivated political leadership (Centeno et al. 2017).

[5] See, *inter alia*, Healy and Malhotra 2009; Gailmard and Patty 2019.

[6] Hossain (2017) provides evidence of this dynamic in the aftermath of the 1974 Bangladesh famine.

I conclude with a discussion of case selection and the qualitative, medium-N case methodology used in this study, before providing background on the country and subnational cases considered here.

1.1 Natural Hazards, Disasters, and Preparedness

Natural hazards are rare or, at the very least, unpredictable events that can threaten lives and infrastructure. The most commonly occurring natural hazards are earthquakes, floods, droughts, tropical storms, and tsunamis. These hazards are typically divided into rapid onset (e.g. earthquake or tropical storm) and slow onset (e.g. drought). A natural hazard becomes a disaster when an area affected by the hazard is unable to respond in a sufficient manner, resulting in economic and, possibly, human and animal losses.

The threat of natural hazards seems clear from news reports of hurricanes, drought, and floods around the world. But how substantial are these threats in reality? As I discuss in greater detail, measuring the magnitude of a natural hazard is difficult due to a lack of valid measurement instruments that can indicate the strength of a hazard apart from its effects. For current purposes, I use share of the population "affected" by a hazard as an indicator of magnitude, which can be held constant across different types of hazards. Using data from EM-DAT – the international disaster database – I show in Table 1 the share of the population in each continent affected by natural hazards over the period 2005–2014.[7] These data highlight that the threat of hazards exists across the globe, but is particularly significant in Africa, Asia, and the Americas.

Evidence also suggests that the threat of hazards has increased in recent years, particularly with changing meteorological dynamics due to climate

Table 1 Variation in populations affected by natural hazards, 2005–2014[8]

Continent	Annual Average Individuals Affected	Percent of Total Population Affected over Entire Period
Africa	16,355,161	15.7%
Asia	147,395,737	35.0%
Europe	722,566	1.0%
Oceania	182,856	5.0%
Americas	11,594,451	12.4%

[7] Note that this measure may double count individuals affected by multiple hazards over this period, but is nonetheless the most consistent measure across hazards and all continents.
[8] Natural hazard data from EM-DAT and 2010 population data from UN-DESA.

change. Predicting the character of such threats is becoming more difficult. A recent study, also drawing on EM-DAT data, found that the occurrence of natural disasters globally had increased ten times over the period from 1960 to 2019 (IEP 2020). These figures may also undercount the occurrence of natural hazards, as preparedness efforts over this same period have played at least some role in reducing the likelihood of a hazard converting to a natural disaster.

Given these threats, what can be done to protect communities and individuals from natural hazards? Government and private sector efforts to deal with natural hazards take many forms, but are typically categorized as response, preparedness, or risk reduction. Response efforts happen at the time or after a hazard occurs, to minimize the damages and attempt to prevent a hazard from becoming a disaster. Preparedness efforts are focused on ensuring that there are programs in place to minimize the risks in advance of an impending hazard (such as evacuations) and improve the ability to respond when the hazard occurs (such as building shelters and conducting mock drills). Risk reduction instead emphasizes changing ongoing practices to reduce the fundamental likelihood of disasters occurring, such as implementing drought resistant agricultural practices. I consider the range of possible government policies in greater detail in Section 2.

Public debates and discussions about the appropriate policy response to natural hazards have shifted over the last few decades from a focus on response to preparedness to risk reduction. In the period leading up to this study, while risk reduction was seen as the ultimate goal, policy recommendations focused largely on preparation, reflecting perceived limitations on preparedness in most countries, especially in the Global South. In this volume, I primarily consider efforts to promote preparedness for natural hazards.

1.2 A Political Institutional Theory of Preparedness

The key theoretical question of this study is: what conditions will make governments most likely to implement comprehensive disaster preparedness policies? I argue that the most thorough efforts to prepare for natural hazards occur in those places where ruling elites are politically motivated to reduce the risks of future hazards and they also have the capacity to design and implement reforms. This is because effective policy initiatives – ones that are both initiated and implemented – require both political support and a capable set of institutions to implement the policy. But when is this the case?

I posit that disaster preparedness depends on two primary variables: elite motivation and capacity. Elite motivation rests on two sub-variables: past exposure and opposition threat. Past exposure implies a record of natural

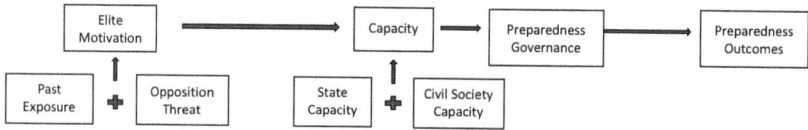

Figure 1 A political institutional theory of preparedness

hazards that have affected a substantial portion of the population in the past. Opposition threat can come in the form of electoral competition, in established democracies, or the presence of plausible opposition parties, in the context of autocracies. Where ruling elites associate the potential for future hazards with the possibility of threats to their continued control, they will be motivated to engage in preparedness to reduce this threat.

Capacity depends on the government, and most significantly the bureaucracy, having the ability to develop and coordinate plans for disaster preparedness. The implementation of disaster preparedness initiatives may involve government actors and/or civil society, but how these programs are governed depends on the relative strength of different actors. The most successful outcomes will be observed where the state effectively leads the coordination of these efforts. Figure 1 summarizes this logic and I now examine each of these variables in greater detail.

1.2.1 Elite Motivation

I begin from the expectation that countries which have faced greater hazards in the past will prepare more in the future. This idea is not new (Fox and Weelden 2015), but I offer a more nuanced and comprehensive explanation for why this is the case. Existing work highlights an empirical correlation between past hazards and preparation but does not sufficiently identify the causal mechanism linking exposure to greater preparedness (Keefer et al. 2011; Hsiang and Narita 2012). Do incumbent governments view natural hazards as a threat to their economic performance (World Bank 2009; Hsiang and Jina 2014)? Do they perceive natural hazards as a potential cause of conflict (Hsiang et al. 2013)?

I suggest instead that ruling elites anticipate a potential threat to their incumbency when citizens can observe the *preparedness counterfactual*. If an individual has not faced a hazard in the past, as in places that experience these events rarely, they will have little ability to separate the quality of preparedness efforts from the intensity of the hazard itself. In other words, because the effects of a hazard are endogenous to preparedness efforts, someone without past experience of a similar event will be unable to gauge the value of existing investments to their or the broader welfare. These individuals cannot conceive of the preparedness counterfactual at the time of a natural shock: "what would have been the impact of a disaster in the absence of preparedness spending?" (Healy and Malhotra 2009: 389).

In contrast, those individuals who have previously been affected by a natural hazard are able to evaluate the quality of preparedness efforts at the time of a future hazard – the counterfactual to what would have happened without preparedness – and can use this information to evaluate the quality of incumbent politician performance. This expectation contrasts with the idea that individuals cannot observe and evaluate preparedness programs, relative to disaster response (Healy and Malhotra 2009; Gailmard and Patty 2019): where individuals have previously experienced a failure to prepare, I posit that they will be able to evaluate the quality of preparedness efforts at the time of a future hazard.

Even if we assume that individuals have no ability to observe the actual policy changes that have occurred, in the form of disaster preparedness, otherwise similar individuals may still differ in the interpretation of their current welfare based on a comparison between the effects of past and current natural hazards. An individual who has been exposed to a natural disaster in the past, particularly one in which the government was ill-prepared, will have different expectations for the likely outcomes of a subsequent hazard. If the results of that hazard are better than in the past, then they are likely to have a higher estimate of their current welfare than someone who had not been exposed to a disaster in the past and so has much different expectations about the effect that a hazard would have on their wellbeing.

This supposition is in line with qualitative evidence regarding the behavior of individuals who were and were not exposed to a significant previous hazard at the time of a new hazard. In India's Odisha state, which has a history of tropical storms, a severe cyclone in 2013 affected areas that had and had not been exposed to a similarly intense cyclone in 1999. Officials involved in evacuation efforts at the time noted that those individuals living in areas that had previously been affected were easily evacuated multiple days in advance, while those who had not been hit by earlier cyclones were considerably more reluctant to evacuate and, in the end, some forced evacuations were necessary in these regions (Odisha State Government Official #2 2014). If behavior at the time of the cyclone is associated with differing past exposures to natural hazards, then we might believe that other kinds of behaviors, such as voting, may also exhibit these differences.

Politicians who are knowledgeable about past hazard exposure can then anticipate this future evaluation and incorporate it into their policymaking decision calculus (Bussell 2017). The opportunity to observe multiple shocks over time implies that once a natural hazard has occurred, politicians may assume that at least some proportion of voters will be able to estimate the preparedness counterfactual based on their experience with this shock. In this sense, past experience of disasters changes the information available to a segment of voters, making them more competent at evaluating the perform-ance of the incumbent than their non-disaster-exposed peers. As a result, the perceived electoral value of preparedness may increase, making preparedness activities more compelling as an electoral strategy than was previously the case. Investment in disaster preparedness, then, becomes a strategic electoral move on the part of incumbent elites, to increase the chances of retaining power in the face of a future hazard.

The relevance of this calculation to preparedness policies, however, depends on whether ruling elites perceive a general threat to their incumbency. This is a relatively straightforward expectation that politicians in electorally competi-tive democratic regimes or authoritarian regimes with a viable opposition will be willing to implement new policies that they expect to be received well by the public. Even if ruling elites anticipate that citizens can evaluate their prepared-ness efforts, these evaluations will only matter in contexts where those citizens can pose some sort of political threat, through voting, support for an opposition party, riots, or otherwise.

Combining these two sub-variables of elite motivation results in four general expectations for the character of incentives regarding disaster preparedness, sum-marized in Table 2. We should observe the strongest political incentives for preparedness where both past exposure and opposition threat are high. Where past exposure is high, but opposition threat is low, we should still expect to see medium to high incentives, given the risk of instability and negative public response in the face of a future hazard. Where there is a clear opposition threat but low past exposure, politicians will have only low to medium incentives to prepare, as the costs of preparation will compete with other policy areas that may have more obvious benefits to voters. Finally, where both past exposure and opposition threat are low, we should see the weakest political incentives for reform.

Table 2 Empirical expectations for elite motivation to engage in disaster preparedness efforts

		Opposition Threat	
		Low	**High**
Past Hazard Exposure	**Minimal**	Low Incentives	Low-Medium Incentives
	Substantial	Medium-High Incentives	High Incentives

The discussion to this point thus suggests that where ruling elites have an expectation that disaster preparedness efforts are likely to result in electoral support at the time of a future hazard, and where they face a competitive environment in which they would benefit from additional popular support, we should expect to see political interest in disaster preparedness initiatives. To be successful in these initiatives, however, also requires the capacity to coordinate relevant actors who are capable of designing and implementing such reforms. I now explore this aspect of the argument in greater detail.

1.2.2 Capacity

The second key variable in my argument is the capacity of the state to coordinate disaster preparedness efforts. Following existing research, I conceptualize "capacity," applied to state or non-state actors, as the ability of an organization to achieve the goals they set for themselves (Centeno et al. 2017; O'Reilly and Murphy 2022: 1). For a government organization, this typically involves "the ability to raise revenue efficiently, the ability to enforce a monopoly on violence within its territory, and the provision of public goods in such a way that supports the functioning of markets, especially the legal capacity to attain the rule of law" (O'Reilly and Murphy 2022: 1). For non-state actors, this implies parallel abilities to raise and manage financial resources, run a functional organization, and deliver relevant goods to target clients. Such a conceptualization implicitly assumes consistent underlying institutional structures that support and enable this capacity. This is, then, an argument about institutional capacity to support preparedness initiatives.

Substantial work in the social sciences has highlighted the importance of bureaucratic capacity for the effective functioning of government institutions. In their agenda-setting work, Evans and Rauch evaluate the degree to which state institutions exhibit "Weberianness" as a measure of state capacity, considering the presence of competitive salaries, internal promotion and career stability, and meritocratic recruitment (Evans and Rauch 1999). This capacity, they argue, is then linked to the ability of states to achieve economic growth (Evans and Rauch 1999). More generally, the quality of institutions came to be seen as a key factor affecting outcomes of both economic and social welfare (Rothstein and Teorell 2008, see also Levitsky and Murillo 2009).

Related work focuses on the frequent gaps in, or limitations of, government capacity and looks outside the state to identify alternative providers of public goods. In the case of Kenya, Brass (2012, 2016) shows how nongovernmental organizations (NGOs) increasingly play both direct and indirect roles in government service provision, through their participation in governance and in the direct delivery of services. More generally, Cammett and MacLean argue that "In many parts of Africa, Asia, the Middle East, and Latin America, states are unable to provide extensive social welfare services, but a diversity of non-state actors such as multinational corporations, ethnic and sectarian organizations, NGOs, community-based organizations, and families provide and facilitate access to much of the welfare that exists on the ground" (Cammett and MacLean 2011: 1–2). In addition, the role of non-state actors in service provision is seen only to be increasing (Cammett and MacLean 2011: 1–2). These arguments imply that we may observe cases of non-state actors filling in where the state is unable to implement programming directly.

At the same time, it is insufficient to assume that non-state actors have consistent capacity to provide these services across countries. Non-state actors differ dramatically in their size, resources, modes of work, and connections to international affiliates or sponsors.[9] Relatedly, the relationship between non-state providers and state actors themselves is likely to have an important effect on outcomes (Cammett and MacLean 2011), particularly in those countries with significant restrictions on civic freedoms. Thus, variation in the capacity of non-state actors is also likely to affect their ability to play a role in disaster preparedness.

My first expectation related to capacity, summarized in Table 3, is that the governance of disaster preparedness efforts, and specifically the character of roles for the state and civil society actors, will depend on the relative capacities of these groups. Where both the state and civil society are of high capacity, the state should lead disaster preparedness efforts while effectively drawing on civil society actors to support its mission, which I characterize as "State-Led." In contrast, where only the state has high levels of capacity, disaster preparedness efforts are likely to rely predominantly on the bureaucracy in a "State-Dominant" model. Here, when the government draws on non-state actors, it is

Table 3 Expected character of disaster preparedness governance given state and civil society capacity

		State Capacity	
		Lower	Higher
Civil Society Capacity	**Lower**	"Uncoordinated"	"State-Dominant"
	Higher	"Society-Reliant"	"State-Led"

---

[9] See, *inter alia*, Stroup (2012), MacLean et al. (2015)

likely to be only for additional support during times of hazard response, rather than in planning and preparedness exercises. In those cases where civil society has more dominant capacity, a "Society-Reliant" model may arise, with government delegating as many preparedness activities as possible to non-state actors. Finally, in areas with low capacity in both the state and civil society, what disaster preparedness activities we observe are likely to be haphazard and uncoordinated, given the minimal ability of local actors to successfully implement reforms.

Overall, I argue that we should see the quality of disaster preparedness initiatives increase in line with levels of state capacity, where the government is able to direct the activities of state and/or non-state actors in developing and implementing preparedness initiatives. Because the government itself is the primary focus for most disaster preparedness programming, I expect outcomes to be better where the state has high capacity versus cases where civil society has high capacity. High state capacity is also important to ensure that diverse actors engaged in preparedness efforts do not, at best, duplicate work and, at worst, engage in activities that conflict with each other.

1.2.3 Theoretical Implications

The two primary variables in my argument combine to produce a set of expectations about the overall character and quality of disaster preparedness that I expect in each country or subnational region, as summarized in Table 4. A key implication of the argument is that disaster preparedness efforts will be insubstantial where ruling elites do not have incentives to support them, even in the context of high state capacity. Given this, we should observe the strongest performance in those places where there are considerable political incentives to prepare and there is overall high capacity to do so. We should also observe considerable efforts to prepare in those places with high political incentives but where there is more limited capacity. In these contexts, I expect to see evidence of governments making creative efforts to engage in preparedness within the kinds of diverse governance structures outlined in Table 3. In contrast, where

Table 4 Overall theoretical predictions for quality of disaster preparedness given elite motivation and capacity

		Elite Motivation	
		Lower	**Higher**
Capacity	**Lower**	"Minimal Performance"	"Substantial Effort"
	Higher	"Window Dressing"	"Strong Performance"

there is higher capacity but only limited political incentives, we may see efforts that look like preparedness, but these will be more "window dressing" than deep and substantial interventions. This is because the government has the resources available to put forward basic policies and/or structures of preparedness, but ruling elites do not have the incentives to implement these initiatives in a comprehensive way. Finally, where there are lower electoral incentives and lower capacity, we should see the weakest efforts to invest in preparedness. In these cases, we may observe individual and disconnected programs, but no widespread and thorough disaster preparedness effort.

1.3 Methodology and Case Selection

This study uses a medium-N, country case study approach, supplemented by subnational case comparisons, to evaluate the character of disaster preparedness initiatives. The focus of the study is the two continents with the highest levels of threats from natural hazards, as measured by the percentage of the population affected by hazards in recent years: Africa and Asia (see Table 1). The first stage of the study considered Africa, with cases chosen based on a pairing of neighboring countries across the sub-Saharan region. This enabled us to select cases sharing somewhat similar natural hazard profiles while also including the range of natural hazards faced by countries in Africa.[10] The African country cases are Ethiopia, the Gambia, Ghana, Kenya, Malawi, Mozambique, Senegal, Togo, Zambia, and Zimbabwe. The second phase of the research extended analysis to the three largest countries of South Asia: Bangladesh, India, and Pakistan.[11]

It is worth considering whether findings from these cases may be relevant in the broader study regions and globally. In both Africa and South Asia, the cases include substantial variation on the independent variables of concern to the argument. As a result, these findings are likely to generalize to other country cases in the region, apart from failed states. In addition, I expect the argument and findings to be relevant in other regions facing considerable threats from natural hazards, such as much of the Americas. Whether the argument would hold in low threat regions such as Europe remains an open question. As these

---

[10] Both stages of the study were funded in part by grants from the U.S. Department of State through its MINERVA initiative, under U.S. Army Research Office grant numbers W911NF-09-1-0077 and W911NF-14-1-0528. The overall region of Africa was proposed and approved in the first stage and specific countries in South Asia were proposed and approved in the second stage. In addition, because this project was based on substantial fieldwork, countries also had to be deemed safe for travel by the US State Department to be selected.

[11] The initial results of these case studies were published in a set of public reports as a part of two MINERVA grant sponsored research initiatives (Bussell 2014; Bussell 2017; Bussell and Fayaz 2017; Shabhanaz and Bussell 2017). This monograph builds on, but substantially extends, the work documented in these reports.

regions experience more extreme weather hazards due to climate change, I anticipate that this could lead to substantially greater preparedness, given high levels of both electoral competition and institutional capacity in the region, but with potential constraints I consider more in Section 5.

In addition to the country-level comparisons, I draw on a subnational comparison of disaster performance in India's states, as part of a detailed Indian case study. This analysis focuses primarily on four states – Andhra Pradesh, Gujarat, Karnataka, and Odisha – selected based on variations in the core independent variables of my argument.

This medium-N approach allows for a detailed, country-specific analysis of both the dependent variable of interest – the character of disaster preparedness – and the multiple potential explanations for variation in preparedness outcomes. The case studies developed and drawn on in the analysis are based on detailed in-country fieldwork and substantial examination of primary and secondary materials for each country.

The decision to use a case study model, rather than a large-N quantitative analysis, was driven both by the character of data on natural hazards and related policies. At a fundamental level, there are limits on the availability of appropriate data cross nationally. As noted by a joint World Bank and United Nations report on natural hazards, "While some countries attempt to collect and archive their hazard data, efforts are generally inconsistent or insufficient. Specifically, there are no universal standards for archiving environmental parameters for defining hazards and related data. Data exchange, hazard analysis, and hazard mapping thus become difficult" (World Bank and United Nations 2010: 3).

Measurement of hazard exposure is further complicated by "the inability to standardize sufficiently scales for the magnitude of a shock that is being used to measure hazard input" (Bussell and Colligan 2014: 10). While significant progress has been made in standardized measurement of earthquakes, and recent efforts to measure cyclone intensity (Hsiang and Narita 2012; Hsiang and Jina 2014) also offer promise for standardized measurement, these are the exceptions, rather than the rule (Bussell and Colligan 2014: 10). More commonly, measurement of factors such as rainfall offer only very indirect indicators of the potential for flood or drought and measurement of combined hazards, such as cyclones and rainfall, are even more limited (Bussell and Colligan 2014: 10).

In the following sections, I develop measures of elite motivation and capacity at the country level and subnationally for India. I then use these measures to make predictions about the likely outcomes for overall levels of disaster preparedness. A summary of all measures for the included countries and subnational states is provided for reference in Tables 5A and 5B, with additional details in the relevant sections.

Table 5A Summary of all measures – country cases

Country	Natural Hazard Threat			Political Incentives			Capacity			Disaster Preparedness Performance	GSDP per Capita (USD) 1999 –2000	International Aid Commitment per Capita (USD)
	Flood	Cyclone	Drought	Hazard Affected Share of Population	Opposition Threat	Expected Electoral Incentives	State Capacity	Civil Society Capacity	Expected Capacity Profile			
Bangladesh	Severe	Severe	Severe	High	High	High	Lower	Lower	Uncoordinated	Medium-High	1,564	15
Ethiopia	Low/ Moderate	Minimal	Severe	High	Medium	Medium-High	Lower	Lower	Uncoordinated	Medium-High	757	50
Gambia, The	High	Minimal	Low	Low	High	Low-Medium	Lower	Higher	Society-Reliant	Low	673	81
Ghana	High	Minimal	Moderate	Low	High	Low-Medium	Higher	Higher	State-Led	Medium	2,026	87
India	Severe	Severe	Moderate	High	High	High	Higher	Lower	State-Dominant	High	1,980	11
Kenya	Low/ Moderate	Minimal	Severe	High	High	High	Lower	Higher	Society-Reliant	Low-Medium	1,578	78
Malawi	Severe	Moderate	Moderate/High	High	High	High	Higher	Lower	State-Dominant	Medium-High	357	53
Mozambique	Severe	Severe	Moderate	High	Medium	Medium-High	Lower	Higher	Society-Reliant	High	441	109
Pakistan	Severe	Minimal	High	Low	High	Low-Medium	Lower	Lower	Uncoordinated	Medium	1,467	33
Senegal	High	Minimal	High	Low	Medium	Low	Higher	Higher	State-Led	Medium	1,366	110
Togo	High	Minimal	Low	Low	High	Low-Medium	Lower	Higher	Society-Reliant	Low	618	118
Zambia	Moderate	Low	Moderate	High	Medium	Medium-High	Higher	Lower	State-Dominant	Medium	1,535	89
Zimbabwe	Moderate	Low	Moderate	High	Medium	Medium-High	Lower	Higher	Society-Reliant	Low-Medium	1,548	106

Notes: The natural hazard threat profile for each state includes the three major hazard types faced by states in the study: flood, cyclone, and drought, and is based on country case reports, supplemented by data from the Global Risk Data Platform, UNEP/GRID-Europe, and Chakrabarti 2019. The threat scoring range used here is: Minimal – Low – Moderate – High – Severe.

Table 5B Summary of all measures – Indian states

| State | Natural Hazard Threat | | | | Political Incentives | | Capacity | | | | GSDP per Capita (USD) 1999–2000 |
	Flood	Cyclone	Drought	Hazard Affected Share of Population	Opposition Threat	Expected Electoral Incentives	State Capacity Coding	Civil Society Capacity	Overall Capacity	Disaster Preparedness Performance	
Andhra Pradesh	Low	High	Severe	Low	High	Low-Medium	Higher	Higher	High	Medium	16980
Assam	High	Minimal	Low	High	Medium	Medium-High	Lower	Higher	Medium (CS)	Medium-High	13068
Bihar	Severe	Minimal	Moderate	High	High	High	Lower	Lower	Low	Medium-High	6048
Chhattisgarh	Minimal	Minimal	Moderate	Low	Medium	Low	Higher	Lower	Medium (state)	Low	13348
Gujarat	Minimal	Moderate	Moderate	High	Medium	Medium-High	Higher	Lower	Medium (state)	High	21681
Haryana	Low	Minimal	Minimal	High	High	High	Lower	Lower	Low	Low-Medium	24251
Jharkhand	Minimal	Minimal	High	Low	Medium	Low	Lower	Lower	Low	Low	12672
Karnataka	Minimal	Low	Severe	Low	High	Low-Medium	Lower	Lower	Low	Low-Medium	18208
Kerala	Low	Low	Low	High	High	High	Higher	Lower	Medium (state)	Medium-High	21550
Madhya Pradesh	Minimal	Minimal	High	Low	Medium	Low	Lower	Lower	Low	Low	13278
Maharashtra	Minimal	Low	Severe	Low	High	Low-Medium	Higher	Lower	Medium (state)	Medium-High	25543
Odisha	Low	High	Moderate	High	High	High	Lower	Higher	Medium (CS)	Medium-High	11659
Punjab	Moderate	Minimal	Minimal	High	High	High	Higher	Higher	High	Low	27577
Rajasthan	Minimal	Minimal	Severe	Low	High	Low-Medium	Lower	Lower	Low	Medium	14639
Tamil Nadu	Minimal	High	High	Low	High	Low-Medium	Lower	Lower	Low	High	21502
Uttar Pradesh	Moderate	Minimal	Low	Low	High	Low-Medium	Lower	Higher	Low	Low	10539
Uttarakhand	Minimal	Minimal	High	High	Medium	Low	Lower	Higher	Medium (CS)	Medium	15061
West Bengal	High	Severe	Low	Low	Medium	Low	Higher	Lower	Medium (state)	Low-Medium	16861

* Natural hazard exposure scores based on Chakrabarti 2019. The natural hazard threat profile for each state includes the three major hazard types faced by states in the study: flood, cyclone, and drought. The threat scoring range used here is: Minimal – Low – Moderate – High – Severe.

Table 6A Empirical expectations for disaster preparedness – country cases

		Political Incentives	
		Lower	**Higher**
Capacity	**Lower**	"Minimal Performance"	"Substantial Effort"
		Gambia	Bangladesh
		Pakistan	Ethiopia
		Togo	Kenya
			Mozambique
			Zimbabwe
	Higher	"Window Dressing"	"Strong Performance"
		Ghana	India
		Senegal	Malawi
			Zambia

Note: Countries in the bottom right quadrant should be the most likely to engage in disaster preparedness, while countries in the top left should be the least likely.

The application of my argument to the country and state cases, using the measures shown in Tables 5A and 5B, produces the set of empirical expectations shown in Tables 6A and 6B. I examine these expectations in detail in the following sections.

1.4 Section Overview

The remainder of this Element proceeds in the following manner. In the next section, I provide a detailed discussion of the analytic framework used to measure disaster preparedness and present the findings for preparedness in the country and subnational cases. I also present evidence showing that the primary existing arguments for the presence of, and variation in, disaster preparedness are insufficient for explaining observed variation in this detailed measure of preparedness.

Section 3 moves to analysis of elite motivation, considering both the character of past exposure to natural hazards in a country – as an indicator of the potential for observing the preparedness counterfactual – and the character of opposition threat. I present measures of these concepts and evaluate the argument based on qualitative discussion of India and examples from additional country cases.

In Section 4, I discuss in greater detail my argument for the importance of capacity in shaping disaster preparedness outcomes. I then present my measurement strategy for capacity and evaluate my theoretical expectations for the relevance of capacity to the character of disaster preparedness governance in the cases.

Table 6B Theoretical expectations for disaster preparedness – Indian states (cases in bold)

		Political Incentives	
		Lower[12]	**Higher**
Capacity	**Lower**	"Minimal Performance"	"Substantial Effort"
		Jharkhand	Assam
		Karnataka	Bihar
		Madhya Pradesh	Haryana
		Maharashtra	Kerala
		Rajasthan	**Odisha**
		Tamil Nadu	Uttarakhand
		Uttar Pradesh	
	Higher	"Window Dressing"	"Strong Performance"
		Andhra Pradesh	**Gujarat**
		Chhattisgarh	Punjab
		West Bengal	

Note: Case states shown in bold. States in the bottom right quadrant should be the most likely to engage in disaster preparedness, while countries in the top left should be the least likely.

The final section offers a combined analysis to assess the overall findings and provides concluding thoughts. Here, I evaluate the ability of my argument to predict not only the character of disaster preparedness initiatives in terms of political support and institutional structures, but also the overall success of achieving disaster preparedness goals. I end with a consideration of what these findings entail for the future of disaster preparedness globally, particularly in the wake of climate change.

2 Assessing Preparedness

The motivating puzzle of this Element is the presence of, and variation in, disaster preparedness initiatives across a range of countries in the Global South. This section discusses the empirical approach taken in the study and documents the empirical variation that occurs in the country and state case studies. In the final section, I also provide evidence suggesting that existing explanations for disaster preparedness are insufficient for explaining the outcomes discussed here.

---

[12] All of India's states have relatively high electoral competition. This categorization focuses on past exposure and frequency of ruling government changes in the period preceding the study.

2.1 Empirical Approach – a Measurement Framework for Disaster Preparedness

The concept of disaster preparedness refers to the range of efforts that prepare for, and can reduce the effects of, natural hazards, with the potential to prevent a hazard from evolving into a natural disaster. This includes, generally, activities that reduce risks in wake of an anticipated hazard as well as programs that increase the efficiency of response to hazards when they occur. This can comprise a wide range of actions, which makes effective measurement of disaster preparedness an important task of this project.

As discussed in Section 1, it is difficult to develop standardized measures of disaster preparedness at the country level based on available hazard or past exposure data. Given this obstacle, I take a different approach in this study, which is to develop an index measure based on highly detailed analysis guided by a single evaluation framework. In other words, I compare the performance of each country and state case on the set of international standards for disaster preparedness that was in place at the time of the study. These standards are known as the Hyogo Framework and were adopted in 2005 at the World Conference on Disaster Reduction. The Framework was used to structure disaster-related policy efforts in the period 2005–2015.[13]

These standards for disaster preparedness are focused on "priority" areas, which I refer to here as components of preparedness. For each component, examples of possible preparedness activities and outcomes serve as measures for evaluating performance in the cases. These components of preparedness, and measures of their presence, shown in Table 7, emphasize establishing a strong institutional foundation for disaster risk reduction, understanding local risk, minimizing risks, building a culture of safety and resilience, and strengthening disaster preparedness at all levels.

2.2 Case Performance on Disaster Preparedness

Each country and subnational state in this study was evaluated against the measures of disaster preparedness components laid out in Table 7. In this section, I review the performance of the country and subnational cases. Table 8A summarizes each country's performance relative to the other countries in the study, grouped into low, medium, and high performance on achieving the goals of each component. For India, Table 8B offers a breakdown of subnational performance in India's eighteen largest states.

---

[13] Since 2015, the Sendai Framework, building on Hyogo, has been in place to guide similar efforts. In general, the Sendai guidelines are seen to emphasize preparedness and prevention (risk reduction) activities even more centrally than Hyogo. The Sendai Framework also adds attention to technological hazards, which is not relevant to this study. For more information, see: www.undrr.org/implementing-sendai-framework/what-sendai-framework.

Table 7 Measuring disaster preparedness

Components of Preparedness	Measures/Examples of Activities and Proposed Outcomes
1. Ensuring that disaster risk reduction (DRR) is a national and a local priority with a strong institutional basis for implementation	- Institutional mechanisms (national platforms) with designated responsibilities - DRR part of development policies and planning - Assessment of human resources and capacities - Foster political commitment - Community participation
2. Identifying, assessing, and monitoring risks and enhancing early warning	- Risk assessments and maps - Indicators on DRR and vulnerability - Early warning; people-centered information systems - Scientific and technological development including data sharing, space-based earth observations, climate modeling, and forecasting
3. Using knowledge, innovation, and education to build a culture of safety and resilience at all levels	- Information sharing and cooperation - Networks across disciplines and regions - Use of standard terminology - Inclusion of DRR in school curricula - Training on DRR for communities and local authorities - Public awareness and media
4. Reducing the underlying risk factors	- Sustainable ecosystems and environmental management - DRR strategies integrated with climate change adaptation - Food security for resilience - Protection of critical public facilities - Recovery schemes and social safety nets - Public private partnerships - Land use planning and building codes - Rural development plans and DRR
5. Strengthening disaster preparedness for effective response at all levels	- Policy, technical, and institutional disaster management capacities - Dialogue and coordination between disaster managers and development sectors - Regional approaches to disaster response with risk reduction focus - Preparedness and contingency plans - Emergency funds

Table 8A Disaster preparedness performance by country[14]

Country	Disaster Preparedness Components Scores					Summary Performance
	1: Political Priority	2: Assessment & Monitoring	3: Culture of Safety	4: Risk Reduction	5: Response Preparedness	
India	High	High	High	High	High	High
Mozambique	High	Medium	High	High	High	High
Bangladesh	High	High	High	Low	Medium	Medium–High
Ethiopia	High	High	Medium	Medium	Medium	Medium–High
Malawi	Medium	Medium	Medium	High	High	Medium–High
Pakistan	Medium	High	Medium	Medium	Medium	Medium
Zambia	High	Medium	Medium	Low	Medium	Medium
Ghana	Medium	Medium	Medium	Low	Medium	Medium
Senegal	Medium	Medium	Low	Medium	Medium	Medium
Kenya	Low	High	Medium	Medium	Low	Low–Medium
Zimbabwe	Low	Medium	High	Low	Low	Low–Medium
Gambia, The	High	Low	Low	Low	Low	Low
Togo	Low	Low	Low	Low	Low	Low

Note: Scores represent country performance on achieving the goals established for each component, relative to other countries in the study.

---

[14] In related work, we give specific relative scores to the African country cases. Here, I revisited the original materials and placed those countries, along with the South Asia cases, into more general high, medium, and low performance buckets, in recognition of the difficulty associated with allocating quantitative scores to these qualitative accounts of performance. In the subsequent text, I discuss the general similarities and differences in outcomes in the case countries both across and within these categories.

Table 8B Disaster preparedness performance by Indian states

State	Disaster Preparedness Components Scores					Summary Performance
	1: Political Priority	**2: Assessment & Monitoring**	**4: Risk Reduction**	**5: Response Preparedness**		
Gujarat	**High**	**High**	**High**	**High**		**High**
Tamil Nadu	Medium	Medium-High	High	High		High
Assam	High	High	Low	High		Medium-High
Maharashtra	High	Low-Medium	Low-Medium	High		Medium-High
Odisha	**High**	**Medium**	**Low**	**Medium-High**		**Medium-High**
Kerala	Medium-High	Low-Medium	Medium	High		Medium-High
Bihar	High	Medium	Medium-High	Medium		Medium-High
Andhra Pradesh	**Medium**	**Medium-High**	**Low**	**Medium**		**Medium**
Rajasthan	High	Low-Medium	Low	Medium		Medium
Uttarakhand	Medium-High	Low-Medium	Low	Medium		Medium
West Bengal	Medium-High	Low	Low-Medium	Medium		Low-Medium
Karnataka	**Low-Medium**	**Medium-High**	**Low**	**Medium**		**Low-Medium**
Haryana	Medium-High	Low	Low	Medium		Low-Medium
Madhya Pradesh	Medium-High	Low	Low	Low-Medium		Low
Punjab	Low-Medium	Low	Low	Medium		Low
Uttar Pradesh	Low-Medium	Low	Low	Low-Medium		Low
Chhattisgarh	Low	Low	Low	Low		Low
Jharkhand	Low	Low	Low	Low		Low

Notes: Scores represent state performance on achieving the goals established for each component. Scores based on data from Chakrabarti (2019), which incorporates measures that broadly cover the range of international standards, apart from component #3, which I exclude here for that reason. This study was conducted in 2017, more recently than the country-level evaluations developed more generally in this study, but focuses primarily on achievements during the Hyogo period. Bold indicates states cases considered in detailed in subsequent sections. The coding rule for categorization is: Low<30, Low-Medium 30–34, Medium 35–39, Medium-High 40–44, High >44.

In the remainder of this section, I present evidence on the dependent variable – disaster preparedness – with a summary of country case, and subnational Indian case, performance on each component of disaster preparedness. I begin each subsection with presentation of the Indian case, to characterize high performance, relative to the other countries in this study. While India has not necessarily implemented every international standard in full, it has made concerted efforts that highlight a considerable dedication to achieving disaster preparedness. At the same time, I provide details on the performance of four subnational cases, the states of Andhra Pradesh, Gujarat, Karnataka, and Odisha (shown in bold in Table 8B), to demonstrate variations in performance within this country. I then consider the additional country cases, beginning with higher performers and then moving to those demonstrating lower preparedness.

2.2.1 Component 1 – Making Disaster Risk Reduction a (Political) Priority

In the best cases, political attention to disaster risk reduction is reflected in the presence of a central government body that is established through formal policies, active in disaster-related planning and implementation, and that incorporates both public and private agencies into its processes. This body should be linked to, and actively engaged with, lower-level bodies that are also officially responsible for disaster-related planning. Government bodies are also actively engaged with community actors.

2.2.1.1 India

In India, central government attention to the issues of natural disasters emerged in the late 1990s. The High Powered Committee (HPC) on Disaster Management was initiated in 1999 to provide recommendations on disaster management plans. As the committee's report notes, their work over two years "followed a highly process-oriented and participatory approach at the national, state and district levels involving all concerned governments, ministries, departments, scientific, technical, research & development organizations, social science institutions and covering more than a hundred nongovernmental organizations. Care was also taken to consult a representative cross-section of urban local bodies as well as Panchayati Raj institutions"[15] (National Centre for Disaster Management 2002: xv). This substantial effort resulted in a detailed set of recommendations covering the full range of actions subsequently put forward as international standards.

Further central government action in response to the HPC report emerged with the passing of a Disaster Management Act (DMA) in 2005. This policy

---

[15] India's sub-state elected local bodies.

instituted a central government agency for dealing with natural hazards – the National Disaster Management Authority (NDMA) – in addition to two complementary central organizations, the National Defense Response Force (NRDF), as a part of the military apparatus, and the National Institute of Disaster Management (NIDM), for research and training. Subnationally, the DMA also mandates creation of state- and district-level Disaster Management Authorities, like those previously established in some states (discussed next), which are responsible for implementing national programs and developing their own disaster management plans. The NDMA is intended to interact both with other relevant national bodies, including the NDRF and line ministries, and state-level disaster management authorities, who themselves interact with the relevant district-level officials (Sarma 2015). The DMA was followed by a Disaster Management Policy (DMP) in 2009 to elaborate disaster preparedness strategies.

These initiatives, while highly comprehensive and indicative of government support for disaster preparedness, have not been received without critique. Three primary concerns are worth noting here. First, while new organizations were created, the responsibility of these organizations relative to pre-existing departments, ministries, and committees has not always been clear. This has resulted in stalled progress in some areas, particularly where there is shared responsibility across departments (Ministry of Home Affairs, GoI 2013, xviii). Second, proposed Disaster Mitigation Funds were only rarely implemented seven years after the passing of the Act (Ministry of Home Affairs, GoI 2013, xxii; Bahadur et al. 2016). It was also unclear the extent to which individual ministries had implemented the recommendation to make clear provisions in their budgets for preparedness and response efforts. Third, some analysts critiqued the highly state-oriented approach of these policies. While non-state actors – both nonprofits and businesses – are discussed in the DMA and DMP as important contributors to disaster management, the specific provisions for, and evidence of, including these actors is minimal (Sarma 2015: 8–14; Martin 2007).

During the late 1990s and early 2000s, a small number of state governments, led by Odisha and Gujarat, launched their own disaster management authorities. Most other states did not implement an authority until after the central government mandate in 2005, including Andhra Pradesh and Karnataka. The content of these state efforts was generally similar, especially after the guidance provided by the central government act.

2.2.1.2 African and other South Asian Country Cases

In other high-performing country cases, there is similar evidence of governments building institutions to organize preparedness efforts and reduce disaster risks. In Mozambique, for example, this body is the National Institute of Disaster Management (Instituto Nacional de Gestao de Calamindades, or INGC), created in 1999, which is additionally enabled by the Master Plan for Disaster Prevention and Mitigation (MPPMND), approved in 2006. "In terms of the national platform for DRR, the INGC is the clear nodal body for managing disaster preparedness and response" (Bussell & Malcomb 2014: 147), coordinating all activities related to natural hazards and organizing regular meetings with representatives from all active public and private organizations for both planning and response.

The middle-range scoring countries on this component also tend to have established national platforms for allocating responsibilities related to disaster preparedness and response, but these platforms are both less likely to incorporate risk reduction and less likely to be fully implemented at all levels of government. For example, "While an institutional framework for disaster risk management does theoretically exist in Senegal, the complicated organization and undefined relationships between actors within the system render it weak" (Agnihotri et al. 2014: 32). In the Senegalese case, "The Directorate for Civil Protection (DPC) is the institutional hub of DRM," but "[d]espite the existence of the DPC … responsibility and liability for DRM is diffuse across several organizations and depends on the type of disaster" (Agnihotri et al. 2014: 33–34).

In the lowest scoring countries, while there may be official bodies tasked with disaster-related activities, there are often not comprehensive national platforms and de facto responsibility often falls to civil society. In Kenya, while the National Disaster Operations Center (NDOC) is responsible for coordinating disaster management, the lack of a national disaster policy limited both the NDOC's ability to expand beyond disaster management activities and to coordinate across diverse actors (Reimer et al. 2014: 112). Thus, while civil society is active in disaster response in Kenya, these activities are often not well coordinated or expanded to include disaster preparedness and risk reduction.

2.2.2 Component 2 – Assessing Risks and Enhancing Early Warning

The second component of disaster preparedness concerns the ability of national governments to anticipate future hazards through active risk assessment, monitoring of potential hazards, and programs for early warning. While there remain limitations on risk assessment, monitoring, and early warning practices in all the countries considered here, those performing well on this measure exhibit a range of tools and techniques for collecting and managing information on natural hazards. In general, these countries have established national systems in place and, often, are partnering with international actors to manage comprehensive programs that account for a range of different hazards in their area.

2.2.2.1 India

Risk assessment and early warning procedures are directly addressed in India's disaster management legislation (Sarma 2015: 16). Subsequent to the Disaster Management Act, the government implemented a multi-hazard assessment framework, which takes inputs from government agencies, including, among others, the Central Water Commission (flooding), Geological Survey of India (landslides), the India Meteorological Department (multiple hazards), and the National Drought Assessment and Monitoring System. A Cyclone Risk Mitigation Project and overall Disaster Management Support System within the Indian Space Research Organization (ISRO) are also contributing to hazard assessment. An overall hazard risk assessment report was also released in 2019 (Chakrabarti 2019).

An area of recent improvement in India is early warning. A combined effort of multiple government organizations, including the Indian Meteorological Department and ISRO, has advanced threat information and warning protocols related to floods, tsunamis, and cyclones, which, combined with other preparedness initiatives, have resulted in substantially reduced loss of life at the time of hazards.

Yet, these efforts are constrained by limited human resources with expertise in loss modeling. Stronger mechanisms for sharing information across agencies and levels of government are also needed, alongside further improvements in last mile connectivity (Sarma 2015: 18–20). In addition, the success of early warning efforts depends on the willingness of individuals to respond to an imminent threat. In India, there is evidence that individuals who have not previously faced a natural hazard can be more reticent about following evacuation protocols (Odisha State Government Official #2, 2014). These challenges must be addressed with improved education programs, as discussed in greater detail next.

Activities at the state level suggest that there is variation in the status of risk assessment and early warning within the overall Indian context. Gujarat was the first state to embark on a comprehensive vulnerability assessment, which examined major natural and industrial hazard risks geolocated to the sub-district level. The state has also conducted detailed hazard-specific assessments in particularly vulnerable regions (Chakrabarti 2019: 133).

With early warning, "[d]issemination of early warnings has been institutionalized in states like Odisha and Gujarat through SOPs [standard operating procedures] and standing orders, as well as the provision of financial, administrative and logistic arrangements at all levels" (Chakrabarti 2019: 184). These systems have been credited with improved early cyclone warning in Gujarat and Odisha, where early evacuations are seen to have saved thousands of lives (Singh 2023).

For risk assessment, Odisha has made substantial progress on assessing overall vulnerabilities. It is also making substantial information on the mapping of vulnerabilities available to the public both digitally and through other information dissemination practices. One area for improvement is in establishing local strategies for real time data collection on risks and active hazards (Chakrabarti 2019: 143).

Andhra Pradesh performs better here than on other areas of disaster preparedness, primarily due to clear investments in multiple forms of risk monitoring. The state set up a cyclone early warning system through the central government's Cyclone Hazard Mitigation Project and developed a forecasting system for droughts (Tejaswi and Kumar 2011: 445–447). More generally, the Andhra Pradesh State Development and Planning Society (APSDMPS) has its own Early Warning Center, which includes automated weather stations, river gauges, coastal stations, and reservoir level recorders to collect hazard-relevant weather data in the state (Chakrabarti 2019: 135).

Karnataka implemented the Karnataka State Natural Disaster Monitoring Centre (KSNDMC), which initially focused on drought monitoring inputs. The center has subsequently been expanding to collect data on other hazards, including rain gauges and weather stations (Chakrabarti 2019: 136). This reflects good initiative on monitoring, but less overall progress in this area than the other three state cases.

2.2.2.2 African and Other South Asian Country Cases

Ethiopia is an example of a relatively high-performing case in which "All assessment activities are government-led and results from assessments must have the government's approval and sign off before they can be released" (Reimer et al. 2014: 104). Assessments are conducted regularly through a government–NGO partnership. Hazard monitoring is also coordinated and cooperative, with a range of data collected by both national organizations and international organizations, including the Famine Early Warning System Network (FEWS-NET) (Reimer et al. 2014: 105).

Countries in the medium category on Component 2 typically had some form of monitoring system in place, but this system generally drew on information from a smaller number of resources and was not fully implemented. Coordination between organizations that could feasibly contribute to risk assessment and monitoring activities was also less evident. Ghana offers an example of a country with an established Hydro Meteorological Agency to monitor weather trends and technical advisory committees within the national disaster management body tasked with identifying and assessing hazards. However, due to limited training of the committee members, these activities have minimal relevance for predicting future hazards. In addition, a lack of coordination between ministries places limitations on the ability of the government to effectively issue early warnings in the face of an active hazard (DeCuir et al. 2014: 71).

Finally, those countries falling in the low category of performance exhibit only token monitoring, assessment, and warning capacities. In Togo, no multi-risk assessments had been conducted at the time of research, with the maps of disaster risk that were available focusing exclusively on floods. A Red Cross–developed early warning system exists, but it is focused on local water-level indicators and not linked to any national-level communication systems.

2.2.3 Component 3 – Building a Culture of Safety and Resilience

Developing a culture of safety is at the heart of the third disaster preparedness component. In this evaluation, I focus primarily on information sharing within government at the central level, as well as educational and awareness programs.

2.2.3.1 India

In India, the National Institute for Disaster Management (NIDM) serves as the central body for disaster-related training and information dissemination, primarily, but not exclusively, targeted toward government actors. This involves multiple initiatives. First, representatives of local urban and village bodies, as well as officials at higher levels of government, are trained in disaster management through the NIDM. The National Platform for Disaster Risk Reduction, established in 2013 under the NIDM, serves as a multi-stakeholder body to offer regular forums for information and experience sharing across government, NGOs, the academy, and the private sector. NIDM also hosts the India Disaster Resource Network, which is an online, searchable repository for information on hazard-related equipment and human resources available in each district.

Within the public education system, the Central Board of Secondary Education (SBSE) has developed a Disaster Management curriculum that is being implemented, while primary schools have initiated activity-based programming, alongside a general National School Safety Programme. University-level programs have also been introduced as disaster management courses and professional programs (Sarma 2015: 24).

For the public at large, educational programs have been led by the NDMA. This includes awareness initiatives such as promoting International Disaster Risk Reduction Day and holding mock hazard drills. The NDRF also engages in local capacity building initiatives, which help to encourage awareness (Sarma 2015: 27).

The success of these efforts could be increased by improved regular communication between various relevant actors and additional efforts to maximize access to, and use of, available databases. There is also a general need to develop a wider base of disaster management professionals and researchers to support overall efforts (Sarma 2015: 26).

2.2.3.2 African and other South Asian Cases

Additional countries doing well on Component 3 tend to have developed programs to incorporate hazard- and disaster-related training into school curricula and community training programs. Bangladesh "has included disaster preparedness and information on early warning systems in the national curriculum of the country" for more than two decades, and primary schools often serve a dual role as cyclone shelters (Shabhanaz & Bussell 2017: 23).

In the countries categorized as medium on this component, field research suggested that most governments were beginning to incorporate disaster-related training at the university level or that NGOs were developing training programs. But these initiatives did not extend to local levels where they would be likely to affect day-to-day concerns of the population. In Malawi, there was a discussion of efforts to introduce disaster-related training into the primary and secondary school curriculum; however, there was little evidence of this in practice (Bussell & Malcomb 2014: 140). That said, universities were already "integrating programs and courses on DRM material in hopes that these higher-level students will become the next generation of policy makers and practitioners" (Bussell & Malcomb 2014: 140).

The lack of communications and training programs in low-scoring countries is quite striking. In the Gambia, there was little evidence of the government using "knowledge, innovation, and education to build a culture of safety and resilience" (Agnihotri et al. 2014: 41). In addition, training of local-level community organizations on disaster preparedness appeared to be absent (Agnihotri et al. 2014: 41).

2.2.4 Component 4 – Reducing Underlying Risk Factors

The fourth component focuses on mitigation and risk reduction, particularly in the context of climate change. The emphasis here is on policies and practices to reduce the overall risk that a natural hazard will evolve into a disaster. Thus, these are efforts that go beyond preparing for what to do when a hazard occurs and instead emphasize ways to change and improve practices to limit the threats associated with hazards. In practice, these are the types of activities that were rarely observed in fieldwork, as most countries are still focused on immediate response activities and, at best, efforts to prepare for hazards. Nonetheless, there are some concerted efforts, especially in those countries scoring relatively high in this area.

2.2.4.1 India

The Indian approach combines agriculture-focused programs, general social welfare initiatives, and post-disaster recovery (Sarma 2015). The agriculture-specific programs – the National Mission for Sustainable Agriculture (AMSA) and National Initiative on Climate Resilient Agriculture (NICRA) – are developing programs that help to make the agricultural sector resilient to climate change and associated natural hazards. For social welfare, a wide range of programs provide resources that may contribute to general disaster resilience. These include the Mahatma Gandhi National Rural Employment Guarantee Scheme (MGNREGS), a combined employment and rural development program that implements risk reduction programs; Indira Awas Yojana, a rural housing program that incorporates disaster resilient design; and multiple agricultural insurance programs to reduce the risks of hazards to farmers (Sarma 2015: 31). After a hazard occurs, the government now emphasizes rebuilding in ways that reduce the risk of disaster at the time of future hazards. All these activities suggest clear attention to the ways communities can develop specialized risk reduction practices specific to their own context.

Three primary areas of concern remain regarding risk reduction. First, it is not clear how the climate-oriented programs are, if at all, directly integrated into programs led by disaster management-oriented agencies. Second, many of the social and economic welfare programs expected to provide the foundation for resilience have themselves faced substantial critiques.[16] Finally, enforcement of hazard-related regulations is seen to be lacking. As one analyst notes regarding disaster-oriented building codes, there remain actors who perceive "that adding disaster resilient features into the structural design may be costly and not much effective" (Sarma 2015: 35). This demonstrates the need for continued public education programs and increases the "need to establish adequate compliance mechanism at local level to implement these tools" (Sarma 2015: 35).

In the subnational cases, all four states considered in depth here participated in the first phase of a substantial Cyclone Risk Mitigation Project (NCRMP), in

---

[16] See, e.g., Gulzar and Pasquale 2015.

partnership with the central government and World Bank. This effort included "improved access to cyclone shelters, evacuation and protection against storms and flooding, strengthened early warning dissemination systems and enhanced capacity of local communities" (Chakrabarti 2019: 148). The program builds on previous efforts in Odisha specifically to construct cyclone shelters in the state "through the construction of link roads, facilitating evacuation of people to the shelters at short notice" (Chakrabarti 2019: 152).

In addition to these measures, Gujarat has been recognized for providing regular grants to the state disaster management authority to implement risk mitigation projects (Chakrabarti 2019: 151). Yet, at the time of this study, none of the four case states had set up the standalone State Disaster Mitigation Funds as outlined in the central government policy.

Overall, Gujarat's relatively strong performance on this component comes from substantial cyclone and earthquake risk mitigation projects, which include introduction of new safety standards for construction and auditing/retrofitting of lifeline structures, such as hospitals (Chakrabarti 2019: 153). In Odisha, relocation programs for individuals living in high-risk cyclone areas have complemented other mitigation activities. Andhra Pradesh performs somewhat better than Karnataka, mainly based on having implemented more comprehensive cyclone and flood shelter initiatives (Chakrabarti 2019: 154).

2.2.4.2 African and other South Asian Country Cases

The primary model of DRR in higher-performing countries is a focus on sustainable livelihoods initiatives. In Malawi, "Environmental and natural resource management is a new and emerging concept at the community level where village participation and protection of nearby resources is the goal of many rural livelihood projects" (Bussell & Malcomb 2014: 141).

In countries that fall in the medium category regarding disaster risk reduction, there tends to be an awareness of DRR as a goal, and potentially some initial moves to incorporate this into policy, but little evidence of specific program implementation on the ground. The Pakistan National Disaster Management Plan includes attention to DRR and how different organizations should work together toward this goal, but the funding to support implementation has been limited. In these cases, the shorter-term demand for resources to support disaster response was generally overwhelming efforts to mainstream DRR into day-to-day policies.

In the remainder of the country cases, while disaster risk reduction may be on the radar of policymakers, no clear efforts have been made to pursue DRR efforts. For example, improved building practices, which can substantially reduce risks in many urban areas, were markedly absent in these cases. In Ghana, for example, where urban flooding is a primary hazard, building codes had not been updated since the 1920s, despite efforts by international organizations to promote better, more resilient, building practices" (DeCuir et al. 2014: 71).

2.2.5 Component 5 – Preparedness for Response to Natural Hazards

The final disaster preparedness component concerns a country's overall approach to preparedness. In those countries exhibiting relatively high performance, the authority(ies) for organizing and implementing disaster management protocols is(are) clear, there are funds allocated to these activities, and there are subnational programs in place related to disaster response.

2.2.5.1 India

As discussed for the first component, India has developed a robust institutional infrastructure, with the NDMA responsible for national-level planning, state governments responsible for state-specific planning and immediate response activities, the NIDM in charge of training and research initiatives, and the NDRF available on an as-needed basis at the time of a natural hazard. Overall, many state governments have also followed through on the mandate to develop their own specific disaster management plans and are allocating resources directly to preparedness activities (Odisha State Government Official #1, 2014; Sarma 2015).

Perhaps the key area of concern for preparedness that has not been mentioned is the need to foster continued mainstreaming of preparedness across all aspects of government. This includes building preparedness into the ongoing activities of all departments, as well as into future planning initiatives.

In the states, key considerations for preparedness include the presence and functioning of emergency Operations Centers (EOCs), both in the state capital and in the districts; implementing a disaster communication system; ensuring that medical facilities are equipped for natural hazard casualties; engaging in scenarios and mock drills; and the preparation of contingency plans. Gujarat displayed reasonable progress in each of these areas, including the use of state-of-the-art communications equipment in the EOCs. The state has also developed hazard-related manuals with standard operating procedures for use in advance of and during hazard events (Chakrabarti 2019: 187).

Odisha has been widely recognized for its improved preparedness levels over the last fifteen years (Chakrabarti 2019: 182). This can be attributed not only to the early warning and mitigation efforts discussed earlier, but also to establishment of clear procedures in the face of an impending hazard, alongside community-based awareness efforts, which have made evacuation and related procedures more effective at the time of tropical storms and cyclones. There remains room for improvement in Odisha in the areas of medical facility preparation and scenario planning/mock drills.

Andhra Pradesh and Karnataka have similar preparedness profiles, with Andhra performing slightly better in areas such as the disaster communication system and implementation of mock drills. In both cases, the states have made some progress in preparedness activities, but have not excelled in any area.

2.2.5.2 African and other South Asian Country Cases

In high-performing Mozambique, it is the INGC that is responsible for organizing all relevant public and private actors in advance of, and during, a natural hazard, and their track record over the early 2000s was perceived to be good. "Overall, interviewees from the development community note the success to date of the INGC in managing disaster mitigation and preparedness activities. As one said, 'People feel that the INGC is there to deal with these disasters and that they are doing a reasonable job'" (Bussell & Malcomb 2014: 145). Key elements of this success include the INGC's coordination of state and non-state actors involved in disaster response and access to an annual, funded contingency plan that reduces the need to request external funds at the time of a hazard (Bussell & Malcomb 2014: 146).

The highest-performing countries also exhibit evidence of subnational programs to support preparedness. For Mozambique, this includes both local community disaster management committees and partnership with NGOs to provide local training and allocate emergency kits in high-risk regions (Bussell & Malcomb 2014: 146).

The majority of country cases fall into the medium-level performance category. In these countries, there is an established central authority that is attempting to make progress on disaster preparedness protocols, but there is little to no evidence of these efforts moving down to the local level. There is also less evidence of dedicated funding to support preparedness efforts. In Zambia, for example, "The national level government appears to have good mechanisms in place and is capable of responding to disasters. However, at the district level, where the national apparatus is not always as robust, it is unclear how well local communities are equipped to respond and prepare for disasters" (Baker et al. 2014: 185).

Those countries with the least developed disaster preparedness capacities exhibit either a lack of capacity at all levels or some central institutional capacity without resources for implementation. In Togo, various government bodies are allocated responsibility for disaster response, such that, in theory,

"The government has the capacity to command the search and rescue efforts, maintain a stock of materials necessary for rescue, and build or provide shelters in the event of a natural disaster" (DeCuir et al. 2014: 77). However, in practice, "it has no budget for DRR or relief" (DeCuir et al. 2014: 77).

Overall, this discussion highlights the wide range of experiences seen across the country cases, as well as within India. What can help us to understand better why some places have successfully moved forward with an agenda of disaster preparedness while others have fallen so far behind?

2.3 Existing Explanations for Variation in Disaster Preparedness

Do existing explanations for disaster preparedness investments, or the lack thereof, sufficiently explain these outcomes? Here, I evaluate four alternative, standalone arguments: (1) governments will not prepare, (2) preparedness will depend on past exposure to natural hazards, (3) preparedness will be correlated with economic conditions, and (4) preparedness will depend on the dynamics of moral hazard.

2.3.1 General Lack of Preparedness

The first argument, that governments will not prepare for natural hazards, is established in theoretical work on natural hazards (Healy and Malhotra 2009; Gailmard and Patty 2019). I provided empirical evidence in this and the previous section that invalidates this expectation, and will only offer a brief elaboration here. The evidence presented in this section on the thirteen country cases and subnational states in India, clearly shows that nearly all of these cases have engaged in at least a minimum of disaster preparedness. In only one country, Togo, and two states, Chhattisgarh and Jharkhand, are scores low on all measures. While these are relative scores, they still indicate attention to the question of disaster preparedness, in the manner emphasized by international standards, across a range of issue areas and policy techniques.

2.3.2 Past Exposure to Natural Hazards

One established explanation for disaster preparedness where it does occur rests on past exposure to natural hazards (World Bank 2009; Keefer et al. 2011; Hsiang and Narita 2012; Hsiang et al. 2013; Hsiang and Jina 2014; Fox and Weelden 2015). While my argument incorporates past exposure into a broader theoretical logic, the existing expectation focuses solely on past exposure. Those countries that have experienced hazards, and resulting disasters, in the past should be more likely to invest in preparedness for similar events in the future, holding constant other characteristics.

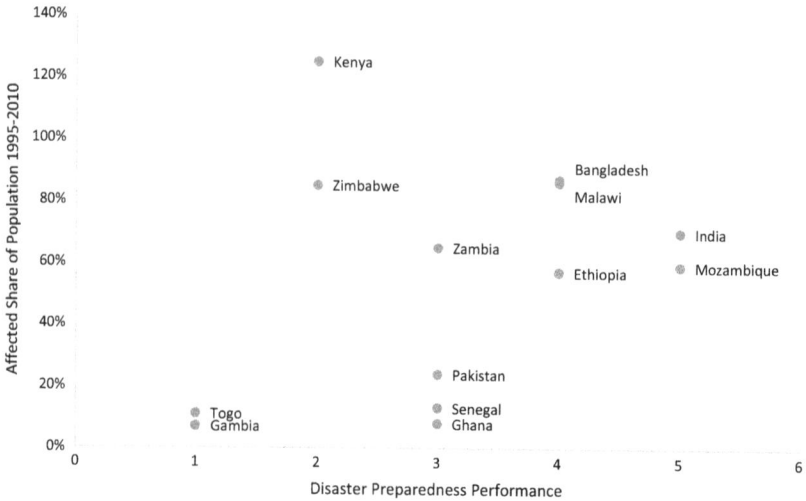

Figure 2A Past exposure is not directly associated with preparedness
outcomes – country cases

I test this hypothesis using measures of past exposure from the EM-DAT global database on hazard events. Figure 2A plots the relationship between the share of the population affected by natural hazards over a sixteen-year period and each country's performance on the international standards for disaster preparedness, as discussed in this section.[17] Figure 2B plots the relationship between the number of events per million people and disaster preparedness performance for India's eighteen largest states. In neither case does the graph display a clear correlation between these two measures, suggesting that past exposure of a population to natural hazards does not on its own predict future investments in preparedness.

2.3.3 Economic Conditions

If past exposure does not explain preparedness, then perhaps it is those countries with better economic conditions who are better able to prepare (Cohen and Werker 2008). In other words, is there a positive correlation between national wealth and disaster preparedness? While there may be some relationship between economic conditions and preparedness, this is by no means clear or consistent, when considering gross domestic product per capita in purchasing power parity or nominal terms, as shown in Figures 3A and 3B. The variation in outcomes is most obvious for those countries with overall scores of 4 and 5 on disaster preparedness. While India is the wealthiest country and also performs at

---

[17] The period is 1995–2010, the same period used in the remainder of the comparative analyses in this Element.

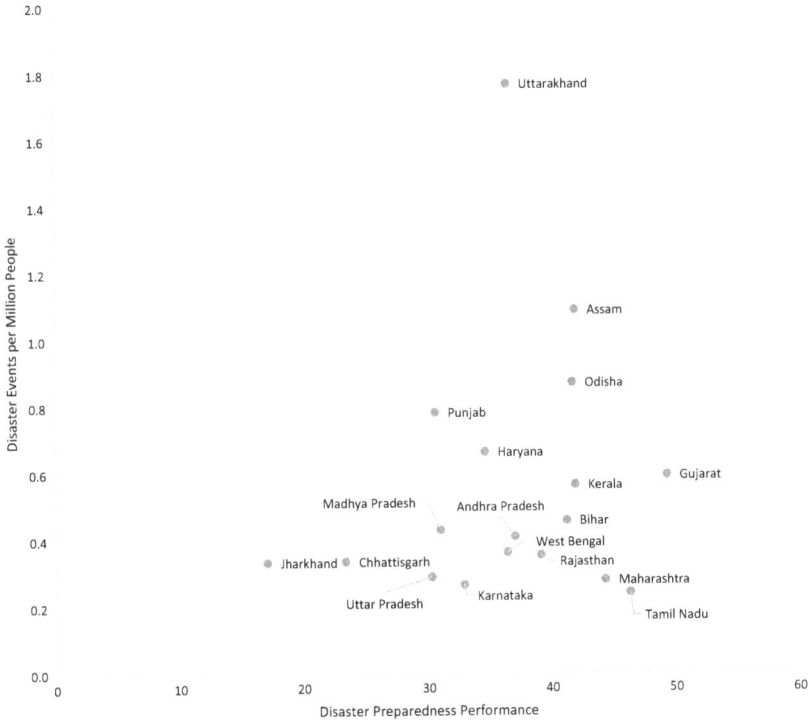

Figure 2B Past exposure is not directly associated with preparedness outcomes – Indian states

the highest level on preparedness, Bangladesh, Ethiopia, and Malawi all scored four overall and are substantially less wealthy than India on a per capita basis. This distinction is most stark for the case of Mozambique, which also scored at the highest level, but is one of the two poorest countries overall in the study. In Figure 3C, I plot the relationship between gross state domestic product per capita and disaster preparedness again for India's eighteen largest states. There is also no clear relationship between economic strength and preparedness outcomes in India's states.

2.3.4 Moral Hazard

A final possible predictor of government investments in preparedness is the degree to which country leaders expect external actors, such as international aid agencies, to provide relief at the time of a hazard (Cohen and Werker 2008). If this type of moral hazard is at play, then those countries most dependent on external aid should prepare the least and those least able to rely on outside actors should prepare the most.

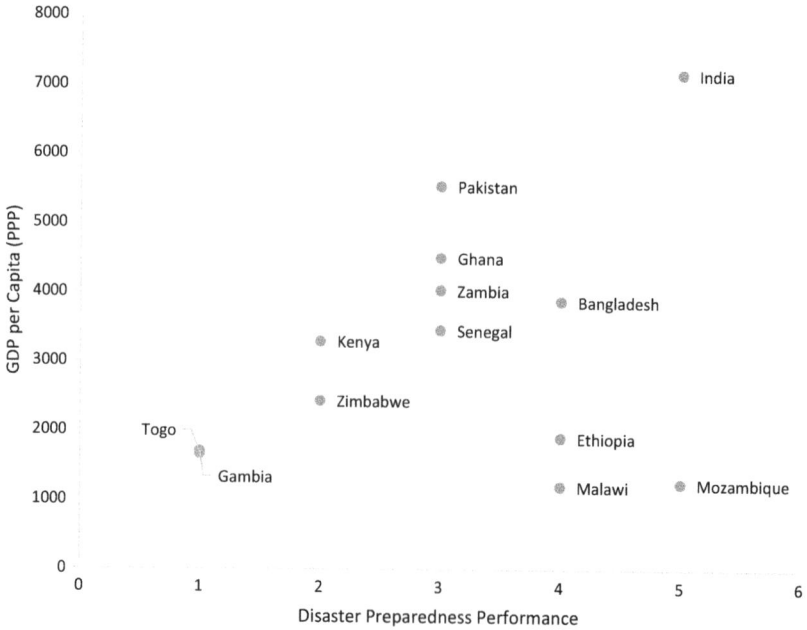

Figure 3A GDP per capita (PPP) displays no clear association with preparedness – Country cases

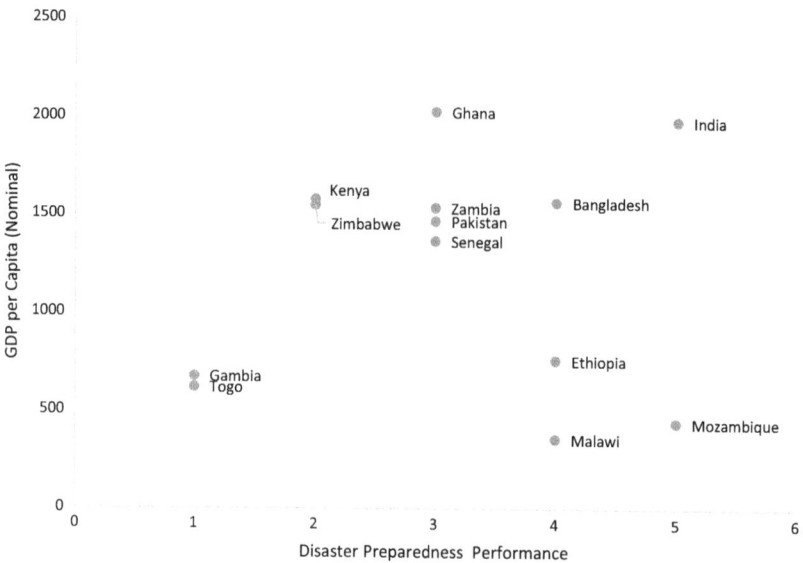

Figure 3B GDP per capita (nominal) displays no clear association with preparedness – Country cases

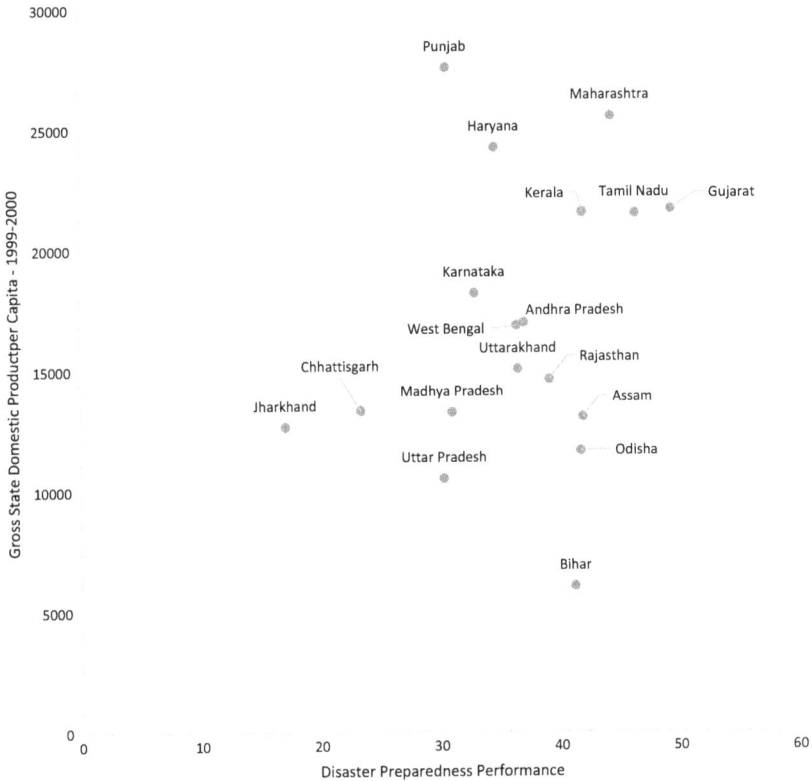

Figure 3C GSDP per capita (USD) displays no clear association with preparedness – India's states

The most straightforward measure of moral hazard is arguably past receipt of international aid. Those governments that are accustomed to receiving aid should be more likely to expect aid in the future. To measure past receipt of aid, I draw on AidData measures of international aid receipts in 2009, standardized by population. As I do not have similar subnational measures for India, I do not test this hypothesis in the Indian states. As shown for the country cases in Figure 4, there is no clear relationship between aid receipt and performance on the disaster preparedness.

Each of these descriptive analyses suggests that there is little evidence to support existing arguments highlighting individual country characteristics such as past exposure, economic conditions, or moral hazard as likely determinants of government preparedness for natural hazards. What this does not imply is that there is no association at all between these characteristics and preparedness outcomes. Instead, my argument highlights the important ways in which both past exposure and access to international aid may contribute in important, but

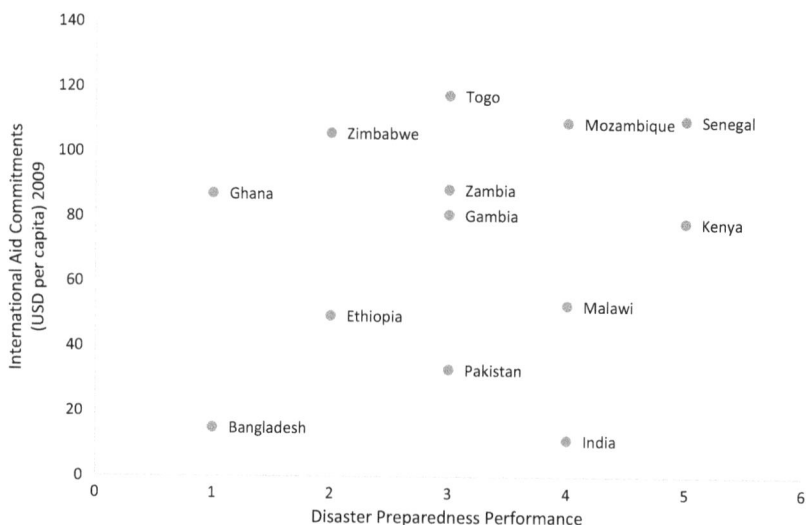

Figure 4 Past international aid is unassociated with disaster preparedness

under theorized, ways in combination with other state characteristics. I explore these relationships in greater detail in the following sections.

3 Elite Motivation to Prepare for Natural Hazards

Under what conditions do ruling elites have an incentive to engage in preparedness for natural disasters? I assume that ruling politicians, in general, want to stay in power and that their choices over natural hazard-related investments reflect this fundamental desire. Where government leaders see disaster preparedness as relevant to their ability to retain office, either as individual leaders, a political party, or a coalition, they will be more likely to promote preparedness policies. Yet, what are the dynamics of these incentives in practice? In other words, what are the factors that political elites account for to determine if it is in their interest to make these investments?

3.1 Elite Motivation and Preparedness

I argue that there are two variables that primarily determine elite motivation for disaster preparedness programs: the character of past exposure to natural hazards and the threat to ruling elites from opposition parties. I consider each component in turn.

Past exposure to natural hazards matters to elite motivation because of the way that it can affect public response to natural hazards. Specifically, government elites should be concerned with whether past hazards have enabled current citizens to assess the degree to which the government has effectively prepared for a natural hazard when it occurs. I argue that past exposure to natural hazards allows individuals to observe indirectly the preparedness counterfactual at the time of a later hazard. In other words, someone who has experienced a disaster in the past will be able to observe how bad things are at the time of a later natural hazard, and thereby estimate the degree to which a government prepared for that event. This should be the case regardless of whether preparedness activities are visible when they are occurring. What the individual instead observes is the difference in negative outcomes from one hazard versus another, which they can interpret as the effect of intervening preparedness activities (or lack thereof). Based on these observations, individuals may retrospectively reward or punish governments for the extent to which they have successfully, or unsuccessfully, engaged in preparedness between two hazard events.[18]

However, whether expected citizen response to future hazards matters to political decision-making depends on the second variable, opposition threat. Political competition is a basic element of states, and all government leaders must consider the relationship between their policy choices and threats to their rule, be they in a democratic or authoritarian regime. This is as much the case for natural hazard-related policies as for other policy areas. Both democratic and authoritarian regimes can face potential threats from natural disasters. In a democratic regime, failure to protect the population from a natural hazard can be fodder for opposition parties. In authoritarian regimes, similar failure can be used to mobilize possible rebellion. Thus, the first factor to consider is the potential threat of an opposition to the ruling government. I conceptualize "opposition threat" as the general strength of opposition elements in a political regime. This can include opposition elements in both democratic and autocratic regimes. I discuss my operationalization and measurement of opposition threat in greater detail next.

Thus, past exposure to natural hazards serves as a necessary but not sufficient condition for substantial elite motivation to support disaster preparedness. We will see the lowest motivation to prepare in places without significant past exposure. But even where there is a high level of past exposure, ruling elites who do not face significant opposition threat should be less willing to engage in preparedness than their peers facing stronger opposition, because the former group is not politically threatened even in the context of a dissatisfied public.

The relationship between, and variation in, these variables, then, generates four probable types of elite motivation for disaster preparedness, as summarized

---

[18] A large literature on political accountability distinguishes between retrospective and prospective voting; see Cho (2009) for an account of retrospective voting behavior grounded in forward-looking behavior.

in Table 2. Where the regime faces a threat from the opposition and the country has faced significant past exposure to natural hazards, there should be considerable incentives for ruling elites to support disaster preparedness. In contrast, highly entrenched elites in countries that have faced only minimal hazard exposure in the past should have little incentive to prepare. In the intermediate cases, elites with strong opposition but little exposure should have only low to medium incentives to invest, while those with weak opposition but substantial past exposure should experience medium-high level incentives for disaster preparedness.

3.2 Measuring Elite Motivation

Evaluating the relationship between elite motivation and disaster preparedness efforts requires measurement of both past exposure to natural hazards and opposition threat. I discuss measurement strategies for each here.

3.2.1 Measuring Past Exposure

To measure past exposure, my politically oriented argument implies that only certain types of exposure to natural hazards should be relevant to preparedness investments. What I expect to matter to individuals' perceptions of disaster intensity and damages, and thus voting behavior, is the degree to which they have personally been affected by past hazards and can then use these experiences to gauge the relative effects of future events. Thus, only those indicators measuring the effects of past events on current voters should be relevant to political calculations over preparedness. This is not to say that voters care only about the effects of disasters on their own welfare, but rather that it is only those individuals who have been affected in the past, and who are able to vote in the future, who are likely to be able to estimate the effects of later preparedness efforts and vote on that basis.

Given this argument, I develop a measure of past exposure based on the number of individuals affected by a hazard. Specifically, I draw on estimates from CRED's Emergency Events Database (EM-DAT) for the total individuals affected by natural disasters, normalized to a per capita estimate. To account for year-to-year variability in natural hazard exposure, I generate an overtime measure of the indicator, based on sixteen-year totals and the sixteen-year average, during the period 1995 to 2010.[19] This period accounts for the ten years prior to the adoption of international standards under the Hyogo Protocol

---

[19] The five-year period for the African countries is 2007–2011 and for the Asian countries is 2010–2014, as was used for indicators of capacity. These years align with the five years prior to our field research in each region.

and the first six years of the implementation period. The logic here is to consider any hazards that viably affected adults who would be politically relevant during the policymaking period under consideration. My preferred measure is the total affected individuals over the sixteen-year period (per capita), as this is the best indicator of the total number of individuals who have recently been affected (even if some are doubled counted, as these individuals may be even more responsive to disaster-related policies).

I also use a secondary measure to evaluate exposure at the subnational level in India. Unfortunately, because many events cross state boundaries, per state data on the number of affected individuals for each hazard event is not available in the EM-DAT database. As an alternative, I consider the absolute number of events that occurred in a state over the same period, and develop a population normalized measure (events per one million people) to compare past exposure in the Indian states.

3.2.2 Measuring Opposition Threat

Effective measurement of opposition threat can depend on the nature of the regime. Given the range of regime types included in this study, it is necessary to consider the differing types of opposition faced by ruling elites in electoral democracies versus autocracies. To do so, I divide the case countries first based on regime type and then apply relevant measures of opposition threat to each subset of countries.

There are a range of techniques for measuring the level of democracy, or lack thereof. Here, I am most concerned with whether a country operates as a viable electoral democracy or not, where electoral democracy is understood as a country with a free and fair electoral system, political competition, and protection of basic civil liberties. This is a "procedural minimum" conceptualization of democracy (Collier & Levitsky 1997: 434). The Freedom House Electoral Democracy indicator maps well to this conceptualization, as it incorporates measures of civil liberties, political rights, and the character of the political process. I combine this measure with information from a prominent dataset on autocratic regime transitions, which codes periods of autocratic and democratic rule (Geddes, Wright, and Frantz 2014). A regime is coded as autocratic if the leader(s) came to power by undemocratic means, if the leader(s) came to power by democratic means but then changed institutional rules to limit future electoral competition, or the military effectively interfered in democratic elections (Geddes, Wright, and Frantz 1994: 317).

For those cases coded as democracies, I measure opposition threat as a function of electoral competition. Where electoral competition is higher, there is a greater threat to the ruling regime from the opposition. I use the Legislative Index of Electoral Competitiveness indicator from the Database of Political Institutions, which codes the number of seats held in the national legislature by the largest party relative to other parties. For democracies, the relative scores are 5: only one party won seats, 6: multiple parties won seats, but one party received more than 75 percent of seats; and 7: the largest party won fewer than 75 percent of seats. I consider a score of 5 low competition, 6 medium competition, and 7 high competition.

For subnational units in India, the same measures of electoral competition and capacity are unavailable or less informative in their application. For electoral competition, all 18 major states are coded as 7, highly competitive, during the electoral terms from approximately 1995–2010 (51 election cycles),[20] other than one term in one state. Thus, a better measure would be whether the ruling government changed during the same period, which encompassed the opportunity for up to three changes in ruling government. Here, in two states (including one that held only two elections) there was no change in government, in five there was one change (including the other two newly formed states that held two elections each), in five the ruling government changed twice, and in the remaining six the government changed in all three elections. I code as highly competitive those states where the ruling party(ies) changed at least twice and medium competitive the remaining states, with the recognition that a reasonably high level of electoral competition appears in every state during this period.

An additional note on electoral competition, perhaps better described as political alliance, concerns the role of party politics at the state and central levels. There is evidence that central governments in India privilege the state governments led by their party (Khemani 2003; Panda 2016). Thus, state governments might be expected to be more likely to implement policies put forward by their party at the national level, to maximize potential benefits from that specific policy. For that reason, I also draw attention in the case discussion to whether the party that implemented a disaster preparedness program in a state was the same as the party that promoted the initiative in the central government.

For autocracies, it is somewhat less straightforward to measure opposition strength. Here, I draw on a new measure of Autocratic Party Strength developed by Self (2022), which considers the degree to which the party is in control at the local level as well as centrally. Self's primary measure is an overall indicator of the strength of all parties in a country. To estimate the relative strength of the opposition, he draws on a second measure of constraints on the opposition,

---

[20] Three states – Chhattisgarh, Jharkhand, and Uttarakhand – were created during this period and so only held two elections, rather than three.

Table 9 Anticipated opposition threat in autocratic regimes

		Autocratic Party Strength	
		Low	**High**
Opposition Party Constraints[21]	**Low**	Medium Threat	High Threat
	High	Minimal Threat	Minimal Threat

based on the assumption that where parties are strong in general but there are significant constraints on the opposition, the measure of party strength should be generally measuring strength of the ruling party, not the opposition. I use the same combination of these two measures to estimate opposition threat, as shown in Table 9. The logic of these predictions is as follows: where party strength is high and constraints are high, there is a strong ruling party with little viable competition. Where party strength is high and constraints are low, there is significant risk of competition from strong opposition parties. Where overall party strength is low, but constraints on the opposition are high, there should also be minimal opposition threat. Finally, where overall party strength is low, but constraints are also low, there is at least some chance an opposition might emerge to threaten ruling elites.

3.2.3 Application of the Measurement Framework

By applying the past natural hazard exposure measure to the country cases, I estimate the affected share of population summed over a sixteen-year period to range from 7 percent to 125 percent. The annual average affected share of the population ranges from 0.4 percent to 8 percent. For the purposes of categorization, I categorize countries as having low past exposure if their total affected population is <25 percent and/or their average annual affected population is <4 percent. The categorization of country cases based on this measure is shown in Table 10A.

Within India, states ranged from having experienced between 0.2 hazard events per million people and 1.8 events. I categorize states as having high past exposure if they experienced 0.5 or more events per million inhabitants. The coding of Indian states according to this measure is shown in Table 10B.

For opposition threat, four countries among the cases are clear electoral democracies – Ghana, India, Malawi, and Senegal – while eight others are classified as autocracies – Bangladesh, Ethiopia, Gambia, Mozambique,

---

[21] In the Self dataset, a high score (closer to 1) on Opposition Party Constraints indicates a *lower* level of constraints. For clarity of presentation, I reverse that labeling here, such that "high" for OPC indicates a high level of constraints on opposition parties.

Table 10A Past exposure – country cases (effected share of population % – total 1995–2010)

Lower Exposure	Higher Exposure
Senegal (13)	Bangladesh (87)
Gambia, The (7)	**India (70)**
Ghana (8)	**Kenya (125)**
Togo (11)	**Malawi (86)**
Pakistan (24)	Ethiopia (57)
	Mozambique (59)
	Zambia (65)
	Zimbabwe (85)

Note: Democracies in bold.

Table 10B Subnational past exposure – Indian states (events per million people)

Lower Exposure	Higher Exposure
Andhra Pradesh (0.4)	Uttarakhand (1.8)
Madhya Pradesh (0.4)	Assam (1.1)
Rajasthan (0.4)	**Odisha (0.9)**
West Bengal (0.4)	Punjab (0.8)
Chhattisgarh (0.3)	Haryana (0.7)
Jharkhand (0.3)	**Gujarat (0.6)**
Karnataka (0.3)	Kerala (0.6)
Maharashtra (0.3)	Bihar (0.5)
Uttar Pradesh (0.3)	
Tamil Nadu (0.2)	

Note: State cases in bold.

Pakistan, Togo, Zambia, and Zimbabwe. There is one intermediate case, Kenya, which is classified as a democracy in the Geddes et al. data but not as an electoral democracy by Freedom House. I include Kenya within the set of electoral democracies based on the country receiving a score of 7 on the measure of legislative electoral competitiveness in all the years under consideration. The Indian states are all classified as democratic.

The application of the opposition threat measures to the country and state cases results in the categorizations shown in Tables 11A and 11B.

Combining these measures of past natural hazard exposure and opposition threat produces the categorization of cases shown in Tables 12A and 12B. My argument, as summarized in Table 2, predicts that the greatest elite motivation

Table 11A Opposition threat – country cases (electoral competitiveness score or autocratic opposition strength)

Low to Medium Threat	High Threat
Mozambique (Medium)	Bangladesh (High)
Senegal (6)	Gambia, The (High)
Zambia (Medium)	**Ghana (7)**
Zimbabwe (Medium)	**India (7)**
Ethiopia (Low)	**Kenya (7)**
	Malawi (7)
	Pakistan (High)
	Togo (High)

Note: Democracies in bold.

Table 11B Subnational opposition threat – Indian states (times ruling government changed hands)

Medium Threat	High Threat
Assam (1)	Haryana (3)
Gujarat (1)	Kerala (3)
Jharkhand(1)	Punjab (3)
Madhya Pradesh (1)	Rajasthan (3)
Uttarakhand (1)	Tamil Nadu (3)
Chhattisgarh (0)	Uttar Pradesh (3)
West Bengal (0)	**Andhra Pradesh (2)**
	Bihar (2)
	Karnataka (2)
	Maharashtra (2)
	Odisha (2)

Note: State cases in bold

to prepare for natural hazards should appear in those countries and states in the lower right quadrant of the tables. Elite motivation to prepare should also be present, though somewhat more muted, in the countries and states in the lower left quadrants. Cases in the upper right quadrant should demonstrate a low to medium level of incentives, while the lowest motivation for preparedness should occur in cases occupying the upper left quadrant. For all these cases, it is useful to remember that there are no countries coded as having low potential threat from the opposition, so we might expect to see some evidence of related dynamics in all cases, depending on past exposure. In the following section, I explore evidence from the country cases to examine the extent to which observed political behavior is consistent with these expectations.

Table 12A Predicting elite motivation for disaster preparedness: Past exposure and opposition threat in country cases

		Opposition Threat	
		Medium[22]	High
	Low	"Low Motivation"	"Low-Medium Motivation"
		Senegal	Gambia **Ghana** Pakistan Togo
Past Natural Hazard Exposure (Individuals Affected)	**High**	"Medium-High Motivation"	"High Motivation"
		Ethiopia Mozambique Zambia Zimbabwe	Bangladesh **India** **Kenya** **Malawi**

Notes: Democracies in bold.

3.3 Elite Motivation and Disaster Preparedness

To what extent are ruling elites actively engaging in support for disaster preparedness initiatives and investments? I organize the discussion in this section according to the categorization in Tables 12A and 12B, beginning with those countries where ruling elites should have the strongest political incentives for investing in preparedness.[23]

3.3.1 High Elite Motivation for Preparedness – the Case of India

As in the previous section, I begin with an in-depth discussion of India, to detail the ways in which the combination of past exposure and substantial electoral competition has motivated political actors to prepare. India is a federal democracy with parliamentary legislatures at the central and state levels. Significant policymaking authority and implementation power is delegated to the states, and this includes primary responsibility for disaster management.[24] The bureaucracy, in the form of the Indian Administrative Service (IAS) and State Administrative Services, also

---

[22] Low and medium opposition threat cases are combined in this table.
[23] Discussion of all country cases is provided in the Online Appendix.
[24] Most responsibilities are clearly allocated in the Indian Constitution, but natural hazards are not included in these lists. The policies discussed in Section 2 have accounted for this gap by explicitly allocating day-to-day responsibilities to the state level, with overall guidance and support from the central government.

Table 12B Predicting elite motivation for disaster preparedness: Past exposure and opposition threat in India's states

		Opposition Threat	
		Medium	**High**
Past Natural Hazard Exposure (Individuals Affected)	**Low**	"Low Motivation"	"Low-Medium Motivation"
		Chhattisgarh	**Andhra Pradesh**
		Jharkhand	**Karnataka**
		Madhya Pradesh	Maharashtra
		West Bengal	Rajasthan
			Tamil Nadu
			Uttar Pradesh
	High	"Medium-High Motivation"	"High Motivation"
		Assam	Bihar
		Gujarat	Haryana
		Uttarakhand	Kerala
			Odisha
			Punjab

Note: State cases in bold.

plays an important role in policy design and implementation, as discussed in greater detail in Section 4. However, India's elected officials retain significant leverage over the bureaucracy and should be seen as the primary actors in determining whether new policies are put in place (Bussell 2012, 2019).

In the years leading up to and including this study, India's electoral democracy witnessed robust and highly competitive elections, both nationally and at the state level. The 1990s saw the central government under the power of coalition governments led first by the Indian National Congress (INC) and then the Bharatiya Janata Party (BJP), followed by a return of the Indian National Congress in 2004 and continuing through 2014, when the BJP returned to power. These coalitions required support from multiple smaller parties for the ruling government to retain power. Similar electoral dynamics were at play in many, if not most, of India's states, and the states can provide initial evidence of a policy shift toward disaster preparedness.

It is common for Indian policy innovation and evolution to begin at the state -level.[25] The era of disaster preparedness in India can be traced to the October 1999

---

[25] See Bussell 2012 for discussion in a much different policy arena, the introduction of digitized public service delivery.

super cyclone 05B that devastated the coastal state of Odisha. While cyclones are a regular occurrence on the eastern Indian coast, this super cyclone brought with it damages of a new magnitude, killing more than 10,000 people (Mohanty 2021) and directly affecting more than 1.2 million, or 3 percent of the state's population. This was a shock to both the state's citizens and its leaders. By the end of the year, the state government established India's first disaster preparedness body: the Odisha State Disaster Mitigation Authority (now the Odisha Disaster Management Authority). The agency was tasked with coordinating all disaster-related activities, including preparation, hazard response, and reconstruction. The design of this agency was a model for the national-level policy put in place six years later.

Though the 1999 super cyclone was clearly a motivating force, it was not necessarily the case that the state government would respond in this way, particularly given that disaster management is not included explicitly in the Indian Constitution and, thus, at this time fell under the primary ambit of the Union (central) government, not the states. Odisha was also not a particularly wealthy state at the time, having a below-average state domestic product per capita in the year of the cyclone.[26] What else, then, might have contributed to the state embarking on a substantial institutional innovation at this moment?

I suggest that the Indian National Congress government in power in the state saw this cyclone as a threat to its incumbency. The INC was in its first term leading the state since the emergence of the Janata Dal (JD) as a viable electoral threat. While the previous Janata Dal Chief Minister and former INC member Biju Patnaik had passed away in 1997, the opposition was now led by his son, Naveen Patnaik, in the form of a Janata Dal breakaway party, the Biju Janata Dal (BJD). The BJD was set to face Congress in its first state election in February 2000, just months after the cyclone hit. And while the 3 percent of the population affected by the cyclone might not seem substantial in electoral terms, its electoral impact could be substantial. The ten districts affected by the cyclone contain nearly half of Odisha's state assembly constituencies and India's first-past-the-post, single-member district electoral system frequently sees seats won by a small percentage of votes.[27] Thus, affected voters in these areas could feasibly have a significant effect on election outcomes.

Importantly, the cyclone was also seen as a major failure of state institutions. As one journalist recounting the event put it, "The 1999 cyclone remains etched in our memories as an apocalyptic failure of the administration" (Mohanty 2021). At the time, disaster management activities, such as they existed, were

---

[26] Odisha' state DPC in 1999–2000 was Rs. 11,659 versus an average of Rs. 16,915 for the eighteen largest states.

[27] Information on affected districts in Odisha is provided in the Online Appendix.

managed at the district level but relied on state- or national-level resources, such as the telecommunications infrastructure and weather monitoring. In 1999, these institutions failed, with dire results. "[T]he Odisha government learned about the change of path of the super cyclone pretty late and soon after the state's communication networks collapsed and the situation could no longer be monitored" (Santosh Kumar, as quoted in Mohanty 2021). Even if there had been more advance warning, there were not evacuation procedures and structures in place and the lack of oversight from the state level also meant that there was minimal coordination across districts. This range of administrative failures is seen by many as causes of the disaster (Ray-Bennett 2016).

The incumbent government did not have sufficient time to implement programs whose relevance would be immediately obvious, as I argue this is only possible at the time of a future hazard. Nonetheless, it could do something that would feasibly be understood by survivors to reflect an understanding of *where* the state had failed. This is the context in which it rapidly implemented a new state-level authority with explicit responsibility for coordinating natural hazard-related activities of all forms, including preemptive disaster management activities, coordination of all actors involved in disaster mitigation and response, and reconstruction after a hazard occurs. These characteristics reflected emerging best practices internationally at that time but were unique in India and also echoed the character of failures in the face of the super cyclone.

Nonetheless, when the 2000 election took place, the Congress government was punished by state voters, and particularly those in the areas most affected by the cyclone. A coalition of the BJD and the Bharatiya Janata Party won a combined 75 percent of the assembly seats in the ten districts affected by the 1999 cyclone, while only winning 71 percent of seats in non-affected districts (for an average of 72 percent of all seats).

Erramilli (2008) has described the 1999 cyclone as a "focusing event" for the state government, in that the policy changes subsequently taking place reflected a shift not only in policy, but in mindset, from a focus on disaster response to preparedness. He also posits that this shift was in line with the dynamics of party institutions at the time, which were consistent with the provision of public goods in the form of disaster planning (Erramilli 2008. See also Chhibber and Nooruddin 2004). My argument is different, in that he does not focus on how the cyclone generated electoral relevance for disaster preparedness substantially *after* the focusing event.

The continued electoral relevance of disaster preparedness is evident in the attention to policy implementation and improvement after the BJD coalition came to power. Rather than assume the Congress policy was a failure due to their losing the election, the new government saw it as an opportunity to further efforts supporting recently affected areas. Not only did the BJD-led government implement the disaster management authority, but it also initiated in 2001 a first-of-its-kind Disaster Rapid Action Force as a specialized unit of the Police to be trained and supplied to act immediately in the face of a natural or industrial hazard. This was followed by a formal disaster management policy in 2005 (before the national policy was passed) and continued support for disaster preparedness activities throughout the period under consideration. These efforts are viewed as highly successful, with the state effectively managing large evacuations and other preparedness actions during subsequent cyclones that have resulted in substantially fewer deaths during major hazards (Harriman 2013).

The second state to implement a disaster management initiative with an emphasis on preparedness was Gujarat. As in Odisha, this occurred after a major disaster, in the form of the 2001 Bhuj earthquake. But understanding the policy change process in Gujarat requires attention not just to this precipitating event, but also to an earlier natural disaster, Cyclone 03A, that hit the Gujarat coast in mid-1998. Why did the state government launch its major disaster preparedness efforts after the earthquake, but not this cyclone?

Cyclone 03A caused substantial destruction along the Gujarat coast in June 1998. Across 12 of the state's districts, an estimated 3,000 people were killed and 4.6 million were affected (9 percent of the state's population) (EM-DAT). The state government was critiqued for its failure to notify the public of the impending storm, amid substantial structural destruction across the coast (Rawat 2019).

What was the state's response? High-level officials note that there was an initial exercise to develop a cyclone-oriented policy in the wake of the storm. Yet, that effort dwindled and produced no tangible results (Erramilli 2008: 185). It was not until three years later, in the aftermath of a massive earthquake, that the state government made a clear policy shift.

The 7.6 magnitude Bhuj earthquake is estimated to have killed 20,000 people and affected more than 6 million, or 12 percent of the state's population. Twenty-one of the state's thirty-three districts were affected. The broader infrastructural destruction was also significant, with major damage to roads and buildings in the affected regions.

In this case, the policy response was rapid and substantial. In addition to a major relief effort, the state government of Gujarat launched the Gujarat State Disaster Management Authority (GSDMA) less than two weeks after the quake occurred. As in Odisha, the agency was charged with overseeing all hazard-related activities, with an eye not just to response, but also to mitigation. This was the beginning of a significant investment in preparedness that can be seen today in the state's disaster preparedness programs.

The state government that launched the GSDMA was the same one that failed to engage substantially after the cyclone, so what was the difference? It is not sufficient to say simply that that the earthquake was a larger disaster, even though it arguably was. The 1998 cyclone had similar costs and affected individuals as the 1999 cyclone in Odisha, and yet it did not result in the same policy reforms.

I posit that significantly different electoral conditions related to the earthquake increased the political relevance of natural disasters to a degree that pressed the government's hand regarding the necessity of this policy move. This was the case due to the timing of elections, the character of BJP support in the affected regions, and the electoral risks posed by voters affected by natural disasters repeatedly in a single electoral term.

First, the 1998 cyclone occurred just months after the BJP successfully won reelection in the state and was not expecting another assembly contest for five years. The earthquake, in contrast, happened two years before the next planned election. While still not as proximate to an election as the 1999 cyclone in Odisha, reelection prospects would have been closer to the front of mind for politicians than previously.

Second, the districts affected by the cyclone were in a region of particularly strong support for the BJP, with the party winning 83 percent of the assembly seats there, in comparison to 64 percent overall in the state. Contrast this with the districts affected by the earthquake in 2001, but not the 1998 cyclone. Here, the BJP had won only 57 percent of the assembly seats. This region, then, posed a much higher risk of retribution in the upcoming election in the face of limited policy response. In addition, with more time leading up to the election, there was a chance that initial preparedness efforts could pay off in the face of any additional hazards prior to the election.

Finally, it is significant that all the districts affected by the 1998 cyclone were also affected by the 2001 earthquake.[28] This suggests that voters in these areas, though previously strong supporters of the BJP, would be able to perceive that very little had been done in the intervening years to address the threats posed by natural hazards. This, combined with lower support in the other earthquake-hit regions, meant that the BJP faced a potential natural hazard-related electoral threat in more than two-thirds of the state's districts. A lackluster response was no longer a viable electoral option.

The next major policy shift was at the national level. The central Indian government introduced two major policy reforms, the Disaster Management Act of 2005 and the National Policy on Disaster Management in 2009, during

---

[28] Information on affected districts in Gujarat is provided in the Online Appendix.

the terms of the Indian National Congress party-led United Progressive Alliance. The first policy set out plans for institutions at the central, state, and district levels to provide response to natural hazards. The second policy offered a more comprehensive framework for disaster preparedness and greater incorporation of local and community-based actors.

Why did the national government choose this moment to implement reforms? The perceived need for a disaster policy was not new to experts in the field or national leaders. After the 1999 cyclone in Odisha, the central government established a High-Powered Committee to review the need for disaster management in the country. A highly detailed report of the committee was released in 2001 and laid out recommendations that covered nearly or all of international standards adopted in Hyogo, four years before the agreement was initiated.

When the report was released, however, the constitutional authority for disaster preparedness remained unclear and the states of Odisha and Gujarat were already mobilizing to address disasters at the subnational level. The central government's response at the launch of the report, then, was to delegate responsibility to the states. There was no clear economic or other reason not to implement a national policy, the government simply did not perceive a sufficient incentive to do so. This perspective changed dramatically after the 2004 Indian Ocean tsunami.

The 2004 tsunami, caused by the Sumatra-Nadaman earthquake, is estimated to have killed more than 16,000 people in India and affected nearly 700,000 across the states of Tamil Nadu, Andhra Pradesh, and Kerala, and the union territories of Puducherry and the Andaman and Nicobar Islands. This event is viewed as one of the worst natural disasters in modern Indian history. It was also a turning point for India's disaster management strategy.

The central government's Disaster Management Act was passed on December 26, 2005, one year to the day after the 2004 tsunami. In a government Task Force review of the Act conducted in 2010, the authors note that initially the GoI decided that policies should be only at state level, despite the recommendation of HPC for both central and state policies. But "in the aftermath of the 2004 Asian tsunami, the GoI decided that a central law on disaster management was essential" (Ministry of Home Affairs, 2013: xvi).

A key difference between the tsunami and major previous major disasters was that it severely affected more than one state. As a result, the varying levels of preparedness across the states could have substantial effects on how different citizens were affected. Yet, there was no central government plan in place for attempting to assist and resolve these differences. The tsunami made clear the substantial potential costs to human lives and infrastructure of such an approach.

The costs were also made evident in three electorally important states. The Congress party was in power in all the major states affected by the tsunami, Andhra Pradesh, Kerala, and Tamil Nadu, either on its own or in a coalition government. At the same time, it also faced substantial competition in each place, with strong opposition in the form of the Telegu Desam Party, Left Democratic Front, and Dravida Munnetra Kazhagam–led coalition, respectively. Andhra Pradesh and Tamil Nadu had also both played important roles in the Congress' success in the national parliament. A failure to respond to a disaster affecting such a large segment of the population across multiple politically relevant states could pose severe electoral threats.

The 2005 Act and the subsequent Disaster Management Policy were also designed in ways that suggest a response to subnational demands for increased disaster preparedness support, in the wake of diverse hazard exposure across the country.[29] Rather than developing programs resting solely within the central government, in both cases the policies provided resources to actors at the subnational level, in addition to formalizing central bodies, in a manner that appealed to regionally based political parties in the coalition. Thus, the central government retained overall control of the policies while allowing for regionally specific programming both to address substantial variation in hazards and to enable local actors within the overall framework.

After the introduction of the 2005 national act, the considerations for state level policies changed. All states were mandated to implement their own disaster management authorities to oversee preparedness and response efforts. Generally speaking, states have "an incentive, in the form of federal grants and fiscal transfers, to adopt and implement central guidelines" (Erramilli 2008: 33). At the same time, evidence suggests that such transfers can be influenced by the political alignment between central and state authorities (Khemani 2003; Panda 2016). This implies potentially varying incentives at the state level for implementation. In practice, we see that such national mandates frequently do generate staggered responses in the states, such as with the adoption of the constitutional amendments mandating new decentralized political institutions at the local level (Bolhken 2015). Similar choices appear in the case of state disaster authorities, with a pattern that reflects an electoral logic.

In the two years following the national government's new Act, nine states introduced disaster management authorities, five of which were led at the time by the Congress government. Some of the quickly adopting states had relatively high numbers of previously exposed individuals, such as Assam and Bihar, and the national policy may have reduced barriers to the development of policies to

---

[29] See Chakrabarti 2019: 103.

serve these voters. The first group to adopt after the national policy also included those with low levels of past exposure, but these were nearly all states led at the time by the Congress party. It is this electoral alignment with the central government that provides a logic for implementation in these cases, including Andhra Pradesh and Karnataka.

Of the six states that delayed the launch of their authority by multiple years, in contrast, none were led by the Congress in the two years following the national act. Multiple of these states subsequently introduced a disaster management authority when leadership of the state government switched hands to the Congress, such as Chhattisgarh and Punjab, or, when led by the BJP after the national government switched power to a BJP-led coalition in 2014, such as Rajasthan. This suggests that an alliance with the central government was key to decisions to implement new policy, particularly in those cases that had not experienced substantial recent hazards affecting large portions of their populations.

Overall, India's strategy toward disaster-related policies reflects attention to the electoral risks associated with diverse natural hazards in a competitive electoral environment. Regular experience with hazards in certain parts of the country, and past voter response to these hazards, provides substantial incentive for the central government to provide not only a comprehensive national-level institutional structure, but also to enable state-level policies in line with the specific incentives that exist for those subnational governments. In turn, state governments' actions indicate a similar set of dynamics, in interaction with incentives generated by the federalist system.

3.3.2 High Electoral Incentives for Reform

The remaining countries where I expect to see a strong electoral incentive for reform are Bangladesh, Kenya, and Malawi. Bangladesh offers a particularly interesting case. Within the central government, politicians appear to perceive a relationship between risk of future hazards and the need for preparedness efforts, which may in part be due to the experiences of past leaders. Governments in Bangladesh have faced popular unrest due to severe natural disasters, such as the flood-related famine of 1974 (Hossain 2017; Shabhanaz and Bussell 2017: 13). Considering both earthquakes and cyclones, compounded risks due to increased frequency and climate change, respectively, have been met with new efforts to invest in preparedness.

Subnationally, however, the character of disaster preparedness at the local level seems to suffer from a bureaucracy-heavy implementation model. Local bureaucrats have primary responsibility for implementing preparedness programs, leaving electorally minded local politicians with little opportunity to influence or claim credit for preparedness efforts. "This effectively disincentivizes elected local public officials from following through [on] their commitment to work with communities to tackle disasters, participate in training programs, and understand the catastrophic impact of natural disasters on the most vulnerable communities" (Shabhanaz and Bussell 2017: 30). In addition, the lack of coordination between the local bureaucrats and politicians "creates an information gap whereby the central government fails to maximize the use of local knowledge in mapping and managing disasters, and relies on institutional data rather than high-resolution, qualitative data to develop and implement their plans" (Shabhanaz and Bussell 2017: 31).

Overall, these dynamics suggest that political incentives from both past exposure and electoral competition can encourage disaster preparedness efforts in high-risk regions. Yet, elected politicians must be in a position to play a role in designing and/or implementing these policies for such motivations to generate positive outcomes. Where politicians see no path to benefiting from preparedness, they are unlikely to exert effort and, in so doing, may diminish the effects of otherwise promising policies.

3.3.3 Medium-High Political Incentives for Preparedness

Countries that I expect to have medium to high levels of political incentives for disaster preparedness derive these incentives from high levels of past exposure and low to medium levels of opposition threat.

These countries are Ethiopia, Mozambique, Zambia, and Zimbabwe. In line with these expectations, the incentives for preparedness in Ethiopia derive more from past exposure than electoral competition. At the time of this study, the coalition government led by the Ethiopian People's Revolutionary Democratic Front (EPRFD) was highly entrenched with little viable opposition and was placing pressure on pro-democracy advocates (Reimer et al. 2014: 117). Thus, the government faced little direct electoral pressure that might result in preparedness initiatives. Yet, as shown in Section 2, Ethiopia is one of the higher-performing countries in this study on disaster preparedness initiatives.

While electoral incentives from opposition competition are not a major factor here, there is potential for public dissatisfaction due to a failure to prepare for natural hazards. The most common and substantial natural hazard in Ethiopia is drought, and the risks of food security and malnourishment associated with drought have only increased in recent years. In addition, "Poor land and environmental management and dramatic population growth in recent decades have increased food insecurity and heightened demands for food aid and emergency relief during drought crises" (Reimer et al. 2014: 97). Even without these recent changes, the fact that there are "many people living in high-risk areas makes them highly vulnerable to natural hazards regardless of whether shocks are frequent or not" (Reimer et al. 2014: 97).

This widespread exposure to past natural hazards across a significant portion of the population increases the salience of such issues within the government. As multiple interviewees noted, "Ethiopia has experienced natural hazards and disasters in the past, so the government is currently investing in preparedness" (Reimer et al. 2014: 117). That this response is due to concerns about broader perceptions among the public, rather than electoral competition, was also made clear in interviews. "The government does not rely on electoral success to stay in power, so it is unlikely that they are improving DRM for electoral benefit. But the government may be spending more on preparedness to improve their legitimacy in the eyes of their people and the international community" (Reimer et al. 2014: 117). In sum, the Ethiopian government is concerned with the public perceptions of state engagement in preparedness efforts, rather than any specific threat from other political parties, and this has implications for its support of preparedness initiatives.

3.3.4 Low-Medium Political Incentives for Preparedness

In the third set of countries, Gambia, Ghana, Pakistan, and Togo, high levels of potential threat from political opposition combined with lower historical levels of exposure to natural hazards suggest lower incentives to promote policies targeted toward disaster preparedness.

Ghana offers an interesting case in which observers note a government interest in disaster preparedness alongside the public's unwillingness to adjust to natural hazard threats. A review of the country's progress on disaster preparedness during the five-year period noted that the national government had "successfully strengthened human capacity through training volunteers, raising awareness of DRR in the public sphere through the media, and establishing regional DRR platforms" (DeCuir et al. 2014: 80, FN 295). At the same time, the national disaster management agency, NADMO, faced resistance to more substantial programs for individuals in high-risk areas, such that "when the government attempts to relocate populations to less vulnerable locations, they clash with government officials and often return to vulnerable areas" (DeCuir et al. 2014: 80). This suggests that while the government perceives preparedness programming to be politically relevant, individual citizens do not recognize sufficient risk to make significant changes to their living environments, even with government assistance.

This contrast between policy aims and public perceptions of risk is consistent with a context in which there is substantial electoral competition, but where most citizens have not been directly affected by natural hazards in the past. While Ghana's electoral democracy is not without some issues (DeCuir et al. 2014: 79), it has experienced competitive elections for multiple decades, with regular alternation in political power at the national level. Thus, there may reasonably be an incentive for elected officials to demonstrate their effectiveness to citizens. And in practice, observers note that "Ghanaians expect NADMO and the government to care for affected communities after a natural disaster" (DeCuir et al. 2014: 80). But these same individuals are not so directly affected by these hazards that they are willing to support government investments in preparedness, making it difficult for the state to move forward effectively with preparedness initiatives.

3.3.5 Low Political Incentives for Preparedness

The category for country cases with low electoral incentives to invest in preparedness includes only Senegal. I expect to see relatively little evidence of political efforts to promote disaster preparedness.

Senegal demonstrates how low levels of political incentives can result in a focus on disaster response, rather than preparedness. In those cases where the government has attempted to focus on preparedness, such as in efforts to move residents from high-risk to low-risk neighborhoods, individuals tend not to be ready to make substantial changes to reduce their risk profiles (Agnihotri et al. 2014: 46). On the other hand, the government seems to perceive that disaster response is a clear area of voter interest and that this can be utilized to electoral ends. "The Senegalese government appears to be responsive to the public's calls for disaster response when the failure to provide assistance affects the government's political capital" (Agnihotri et al. 2014: 46) and at the same time, "Evidence from the interviews suggests that flooding has provided an opportunity for the ruling party to diminish the popularity of opposition members in office by withholding or delaying resources after natural hazards" (Agnihotri et al. 2014: 47). This latter strategy appeared to be the case in the flood-prone city of Saint Louis, where flood assistance declined in the year after an opposition mayor took power in the city (Agnihotri et al. 2014: 45).

This evidence suggests that the preparedness efforts observed in Senegal are only minimally driven by political incentives. To the extent that preparedness goals are aligned with strategies to support disaster response, these efforts are likely to gain political support, but broader, programmatic changes are unlikely to emerge from direct political initiative in this environment.

3.4 Conclusion

The analysis of political incentives in this section highlights the complicated dynamics facing political elites when considering disaster preparedness. In Table 13, I summarize my findings for whether observed political incentives for, and thus political interest in, disaster preparedness in the study cases is in line with the predictions of my argument. Countries and states that match well to my expectations are shown in bold, while those exhibiting some variations from the expectations are shown in italics. Overall, my argument provides strong guidelines for examining what to expect in most cases, closely predicting not only the conditions under which we should see strong government support for preparedness, but also where this is less likely to be the case. Importantly, we can see the varying interactions between past exposure and electoral conditions, suggesting that past exposure can generate electoral incentives for engaging in preparedness even where there are lower levels of electoral threat, but the opposite is not the case for high levels of opposition threat in the absence of past exposure.

Table 13 Performance of theoretical expectations for political incentives in country and Indian state cases

| | | Opposition Threat | |
		Medium	High
	Low	"Low Incentives"	"Low-Medium Incentives"
		Senegal	**Gambia** **Ghana** **Pakistan** **Togo**
Past Natural Hazard Exposure (Individuals Affected)			**Andhra Pradesh** **Karnataka**
	High	"Medium-High Incentives"	"High Incentives"
		Ethiopia **Mozambique** **Zambia** **Zimbabwe**	**Bangladesh** **India** *Kenya* *Malawi*
		Gujarat	**Odisha**

Notes: Bold shows cases that match well to my expectations; italics indicates some variations from expectations.

4 Capacity to Prepare for Natural Hazards

What is necessary for the successful design and implementation of disaster preparedness? What determines the governance model by which preparedness efforts are implemented? I argue that high levels of preparedness are most likely in those cases where the state has capacity to coordinate actors relevant for preparedness efforts and those actors, either within or outside the state, have the capacity to design and implement preparedness initiatives. This implies the presence, first, of basic organizational and implementation skills; and second, the application of these skills to the task of disaster preparedness. Importantly, I argue that a country must have the first, in some form, to achieve the second.

These skills may exist in the public sector, private sector, or both. In considering whether countries exhibit the potential capacity to engage in disaster preparedness, I ask both whether the government exhibits a stable, functioning bureaucracy in general and whether there exist private actors – nongovernmental organizations – to potentially complement government efforts. This dual approach accounts for the substantial evidence that actors within the state can play an important role in administration and stability (Hassan 2020) while at the same time those outside the state can also be significant enablers of development in the Global South (Hammett and MacLean 2011; Brass 2012, 2016). The dual role of these actors at the time of natural hazards has been noted in considering the role of social capital in disaster response (Aldrich 2012). The presence of capacity provides the potential for developing and implementing specific programs for disaster preparedness – there are individuals and groups in the country who can design plans for these activities and the skills to manage implementation effectively. Without this latent capacity, even the most motivated political actors will struggle to introduce a successful preparedness initiative.

At the same time, I argue that the state's capacity plays the dominant role in determining how, and how well, disaster preparedness efforts are governed. Effective disaster preparedness is most likely in those places where the state has sufficient capacity to implement reforms. These reforms may be improved by the presence of a viable nonprofit sector that is available to partner with the state, but this is not necessary. Where the state is sufficiently capable, a strong disaster preparedness program can emerge in the absence of non-state actor participation. In contrast, where state institutions are weak and the nongovernmental sector is strong, it may be feasible for disaster preparedness activities to emerge, but these efforts will reflect a reliance of the state on non-state actors for implementation. Finally, where both the state and civil society lack substantial capacity, there should be minimal evidence of effective disaster preparedness, even in the context of a formal disaster management policy. These predictions are summarized as four likely capacity profiles in Table 3.

4.1 Measuring Capacity

To measure capacity, defined here as the ability of organizations to implement their goals, I develop a general framework for evaluating combined state and non-state capacity and then apply that framework to my country and subnational cases. Measuring capacity is a highly contested area of social science, and I draw on multiple existing resources to triangulate measures of both state and civil society capacity. This allows me to establish a baseline for general capacity of the state and private actors before investigating how that capacity plays out regarding specific programs for disaster preparedness.

It is important to note that capacity is not static but can change over time and differ across parts of an organization. In particular, and as my argument in general implies, capacity, especially within the state, often changes because of political will to strengthen the government apparatus.[30] For current purposes, I want to evaluate the capacity of the state and social actors at a moment in time to gauge existing capacity at the beginning of the study. Empirically, my expectation is that effective disaster preparedness efforts will build capacity within the state and/or society, but those changes in capacity are a part of the outcomes I seek to explain, rather than causes of those outcomes.

4.1.1 State Capacity

My country-level measure of state capacity draws from the O'Reilly and Murphy (2022) Index of State Capacity, which is an index of measures from the V-Dem dataset. The baseline measure includes V-Dem scores for "the rule of law, the authority of the state over its territory, the rigorousness and impartiality of public administration, whether public expenditures are on particularistic or public goods, the modernity of the state's source of its revenue, and the universality of the provision of education" (O'Reilly and Murphy 2022: 713). I begin with the baseline capacity measure for the five years prior to the start of the study in each region, 2007–2011 for African countries and 2010–2014 for South Asian countries. I then generate an average capacity measure for each country across the five-year window. The Index of State Capacity baseline measure ranges from −4 to 4 and the average scores for countries included in this study range from −1 to 1. I classify those countries receiving a capacity score of −1 or 0 as lower capacity and those scoring a 1 as higher capacity, as

---

[30] For a general treatment of this dynamic see Centeno et al. (2017) and specifically with regard to natural hazards Hossain (2017).

Table 14A Domestic government capacity – country cases
(five-year average score)

Lower Capacity	Higher Capacity
Bangladesh (0)	Ghana (1)
Ethiopia (0)	India (1)
Gambia, The (0)	Malawi (1)
Kenya ((0)	Senegal (1)
Mozambique (0)	Zambia (1)
Togo (0)	
Pakistan (-1)	
Zimbabwe (-1)	

Table 14B Subnational government capacity – Indian states
(capacity score)

Lower Capacity	Higher Capacity
Odisha (4)	Kerala (10)
Haryana (4)	Andhra Pradesh (6)
Jharkhand (4)	Gujarat (6)
Tamil Nadu (4)	Maharashtra (6)
Uttarakhand (4)	Chhattisgarh (5)
Uttar Pradesh (4)	Punjab (5)
Assam (3)	West Bengal (5)
Karnataka (3)	
Rajasthan (3)	
Madhya Pradesh (2)	
Bihar (0)	

shown in Table 14A. That said, these groupings indicate capacity levels relative to each other, not the global set of countries, given that these countries all sit at the middle of the range of scores and none are toward the extremes.

For the Indian states, there are no established measures of subnational capacity in the literature. Here, I use an alternative measure of corruption in the delivery of public services. This measure is intended to capture the quality of the bureaucracy via the degree to which the state apparatus can direct the behavior of its individual bureaucrats toward the successful and efficient implementation of government programs.[31] The measure comes from a citizen survey conducted in 2004–2005 by Transparency International India and the Centre for

---

[31] This operationalization is consistent with related work such as Evans and Rauch (1999) and Centeno et al. (2017).

Media Studies. Respondents were asked about their experiences with eleven different citizen-facing departments and an overall corruption score was generated for each state (Transparency International India 2005).

Among the eighteen major Indian states, the corruption scores range from 240 (lowest corruption) in Kerala to 695 (highest corruption) in Bihar. Because there is no clear "break" between higher- and lower-corruption states, I normalized the scores on a scale from 0 to 10 and reversed the order, so that the lowest scoring on the corruption index have the highest capacity scores. I then coded those states scoring 5 or higher on the indicator as high capacity and those scoring below 5 as lower capacity. I use this measure to estimate the levels of state capacity in these states.

4.1.2 Civil Society Capacity

Measurement of civil society capacity is not as well established in the existing literature as state capacity. I aim to generate a measure that considers both the presence of non-state organizations and the ability of these organizations to operate within a given country context. In addition, I consider historical measures of international aid.

I first generate a measure of local nongovernmental organization presence based on data from the World Organization of Non-Governmental Organizations (WANGO). WANGO tracks currently active NGOs, so these data are more recent than the other measures used here, but are the most comprehensive available across countries. The per capita measure is based on the total number of domestic NGOs listed for each country and current (2022) population data. The case countries fell into three general categories, which I categorize as having an NGO presence that is Low (<4/million people), Medium (>4 and <8/million people), or High (>8/million people), as shown in Table 15.

The second measure of non-state capacity is based on the presence of international aid in a country. While some aid typically goes directly to

Table 15 Domestic NGO presence (NGOs per million people)

Low	Medium	High
Malawi (2.2)	Zimbabwe (6.3)	Ghana (23.1)
Bangladesh (2.1)	Togo (6.2)	The Gambia (13.7)
India (1.7)	Zambia (4.7)	Kenya (8.0)
Ethiopia (0.5)	Senegal (4.2)	
Mozambique (0.4)	Pakistan (4.1)	

Table 16 Per capita aid commitment levels in 2009, recipient countries (US$)

Low	Medium	High
Pakistan (33)	Zambia (89)	Togo (118)
India (15)	Ghana (87)	Mozambique (110)
Bangladesh (11)	Gambia (81)	Senegal (110)
	Kenya (78)	Zimbabwe (106)
	Malawi (53)	
	Ethiopia (50)	

governments, the ability of domestic NGOs to operate also often rests on financial and other inputs from international actors.[32] Here, I use measures from AidData of overall bilateral and multilateral commitments to each country in 2009, which was the most recent year for which there was data for all countries in the study. I then generated a per capita measure based on populations in 2009. Again, I subsequently place the countries into three groups, following a general sorting in the data that uses the following rubric: Low (<$40/person), Medium (>$40 and <$90/person), and High (>$90/person), shown in Table 16.

In theory, I would prefer a measure of domestic non-state capacity that accounts for the status of civic freedoms in each country. This would help to ensure that any NGOs that are listed as being active are actually able to work successfully. In practice, inconsistent availability of data on civic freedom across the study countries means that it is not possible to develop a measure that takes this into account in a consistent manner.[33]

My alternative, to combine measures of domestic NGO presence and international aid, while limited in its direct measurement of civic freedom, also has benefits. The presence of domestic NGOs may be not only a direct measure of NGO presence, but also an indirect measure of civic freedom, as implied by the ability of individuals to form and maintain these organizations. This measurement strategy also, as noted earlier, accounts for the frequent relationship between international aid and domestic NGOs.

To facilitate a more general discussion, it is useful to collapse the capacity measures into two categories. I collapse the multifaceted civil society capacity

---

[32] See, for example, Brass (2016) in which the first paragraph describes a meeting to interview a local Kenyan NGO that is an implementing partner for a US-based nonprofit active in thirty countries.

[33] There is missing data for multiple study countries in the frequently used sources, including the World Values Survey, Afrobarometer, and the Ibrahim Index of African Governance.

Table 17 Combined civil society country
capacity profiles

Lower Capacity	Higher Capacity
Bangladesh	Gambia
Ethiopia	Ghana
India	Kenya
Malawi	Mozambique
Pakistan	Senegal
Zambia	Togo
	Zimbabwe

Table 18 Civil society Indian state capacity
profiles (NGOs per million people)

Lower Capacity	Higher Capacity
Jharkhand (1.9)	Punjab (16.1)
Haryana (1.8)	Uttarakhand (3.3)
Karnataka (1.8)	Andhra Pradesh (2.5)
Tamil Nadu (1.8)	Assam (2.1)
West Bengal (1.7)	Odisha (2.0)
Maharashtra (1.5)	
Gujarat (1.4)	
Kerala (1.4)	
Rajasthan (1.2)	
Bihar (0.7)	
Madhya Pradesh (0.6)	
Chhattisgarh (0.5)	
Uttar Pradesh (0.5)	

measure into a single dimension by grouping those countries that received a "high" on either measure with those receiving a "medium" on both measures as higher capacity and the remaining countries as lower capacity, shown in Table 17.

For India, I use the same world database of NGOs as for the cross-national comparison. These data include the state where an NGO is based and so can account for state-level presence of NGOs. I then generate a normalized measure based on the number of NGOs per million people in the state, as shown in Table 18. While there is some NGO presence in all states, a few states have a substantially higher presence than the others. I do not have a comparable measure of international aid commitments at the subnational level in India; thus, I rely here solely on the measure of NGO presence.

4.1.3 Overall Capacity Profiles

The set of government and civil society capacity measures enables an overall categorization of countries into two-dimensional capacity profiles, with predictions in each category for the likely governance style of disaster preparedness management, shown in Tables 19A and 19B.

Table 19A Overall country capacity profiles

		State Capacity	
		Lower	Higher
	Lower	"Uncoordinated"	"State-Dominant"
		Bangladesh	India
		Ethiopia	Malawi
		Pakistan	Zambia
Civil Society Capacity	**Higher**	"Society-Reliant"	"State-Led"
		Gambia	Ghana
		Kenya	Senegal
		Mozambique	
		Togo	
		Zimbabwe	

Table 19B Overall Indian state capacity profiles

		State Capacity	
		Lower	Higher
	Lower	"Uncoordinated"	"State-Dominant"
		Bihar	Chhattisgarh
		Haryana	**Gujarat**
		Jharkhand	Kerala
		Karnataka	Maharashtra
		Madhya Pradesh	West Bengal
Civil Society Capacity		Rajasthan	
		Tamil Nadu	
		Uttar Pradesh	
	Higher	"Society-Reliant"	"State-Led"
		Assam	**Andhra Pradesh**
		Odisha	Punjab
		Uttarakhand	

Note: State cases in bold.

What are the implications of these profiles for an argument about the relevance of latent capacity to disaster preparedness? My primary supposition is that latent capacities should set the stage for particular models of disaster preparedness. Specifically, I expect differing alignments of state and non-state capacity to result in differing governance strategies for preparedness, where preparedness exists at all. In other words, latent capacity does not on its own determine whether a country will exhibit disaster preparedness. Rather, capacity serves as a foundation for preparedness efforts and shapes the character of that preparedness where it occurs. In the context of disaster preparedness, it also matters who has the capacity. I anticipate that the most comprehensive disaster preparedness initiatives will appear in those contexts where the state is high capacity and has an electoral incentive to apply this capacity to preparedness efforts, as elaborated in the previous section.

4.2 Capacity and Models of Preparedness

Having established general capacity profiles for the countries and states included in this study, I now evaluate whether there is a clear relationship between these profiles and the character of approaches taken toward disaster preparedness. Specifically, what, if any, is the relationship between a country's (or state's) latent capacity for disaster preparedness and how it approaches disaster preparedness?

I organize the empirical discussion based on the predicted patterns noted earlier. I begin, as in previous sections, with the case of India, considering both the national level and the states of Gujarat, Andhra Pradesh, Odisha, and Karnataka, before providing additional examples from other countries.[34]

4.2.1 India – a High-Capacity State, with Subnational Variation

In India overall, my capacity measures suggest an outsized role for the state in preparedness, with a minimal and subsidiary role for non-state actors. It is useful to provide additional background on the Indian administrative set-up as context for the specifics of the case discussion. The Indian government operates through multiple layers of administrative hierarchy, with leadership resting in the central services. These administrative groups include the Indian Administrative Services (IAS), a generalist branch that runs most departments; the Indian Police Service (IPS); Indian Foreign Service (IFS), and others. Officers in these services are hired through a highly competitive, country-wide merit-based process, and after joining a service are typically posted to a specific state cadre for their career. Once an individual reaches a certain level of tenure and experience, they may be eligible for positions in central

---

[34] Discussion of all countries is provided in the Online Appendix.

government departments, such as the Department of Road Transport and Highways, the Central Bureau of Investigation, or the National Disaster Management Authority. State governments also have their own administrative services, to fill positions at lower levels within government departments. Though not without critique, these bodies provide the foundation upon and through which all government programs are implemented in India.

In practice, for disaster management, there is a clearly delineated set of central government organizations with responsibility for leading disaster-related efforts, as well as delegation of responsibilities to related bodies at the subnational level. Three departments – the National Disaster Management Authority (NDMA), National Disaster Response Force (NDRF), and National Institute for Disaster Management (NIDM) – are responsible for, respectively, policy guidelines related to disaster preparedness and response, active response to natural hazards, and providing disaster training programs.

The functioning of these organizations reflects the substantial administrative capacity of the central Indian state. Take, for example, the NDMA. In most high-level bureaucratic positions in India, members of the administrative services are placed in positions based on their generalist training, not due to specific areas of expertise. In the NDMA, however, all senior officials in the secretariat have previous experience with disaster-related issues, such as having previously worked in a disaster-prone area (NDMA Official, March 24, 2014). At the same time, the generalist training of senior bureaucrats can be particularly useful in a cross-cutting issue area such as disaster preparedness. A key role for the NDMA is to generate guidelines for mainstreaming disaster preparedness in both cross-departmental and regular activities of line departments. Having administrative leadership with experience across multiple departments should enable these activities.

The NIDM, charged with capacity building, takes an active role in developing overall training programs and specialized initiatives to respond to new hazards. When unanticipated landslides and floods hit the state of Uttarakhand in 2014, the institute sent a team to conduct site visits and interviews as the basis of a report on the disaster (NIDM Official, March 25, 2014). Reports of this kind are then used to disseminate information and contribute to future training programs. The training programs themselves are implemented based on requests from states and other organizations, including NGOs. But the programming is offered by the NIDM itself, not through partnerships with other organizations.

In these ways, the disaster management and preparedness efforts of the Indian government are conducted largely without the support of, or coordination with, civil society actors. While local NGOs might participate in specific training activities or assist in response, these efforts are clearly designed and implemented by the state in line with plans and procedures set out in government policy. Thus, India offers strong support for a state-dominant model in a case where state capacity outweighs that of the non-state sector.

Within the state cases, there should be slight variations on this model. In Gujarat, high state capacity with low presence of civil society suggests a dominant role for the government in disaster preparedness initiatives, with minimal engagement of non-state actors in implementation of state policies. Odisha, in contrast with Gujarat, ranks relatively lower on state capacity – scoring near the midpoint of the states – but has a higher presence of non-state actors to potentially participate in preparedness initiatives. Thus, state-led initiatives that actively engage with local nongovernmental organizations are more likely there. Andhra Pradesh is a high-government capacity state, scoring nearly the same as Gujarat on this indicator. In contrast with the other cases, however, Andhra also has a relatively high presence of NGOs. To the extent that there are disaster preparedness programs in place, they should be state-led initiatives that leverage the availability of non-state actors. The final case, Karnataka, represents low levels of both state and civil society capacity. Given these institutional conditions, there should be more haphazard management of any existing preparedness activities.

In Gujarat, there is a highly state-driven preparedness model, as anticipated by my argument. The introduction of the state disaster management authority was done in a manner that focused explicitly on leadership of, and execution by, the state. Indeed, as one expert notes, at the level of state policy, "Gujarat seemed to have dispensed with an institutionalized role for NGOs during non-disaster times" (Erramilli 2008: 88). This approach also prevailed locally, such that Erramilli observed, in Gujarat's village-level preparedness and response activities, "unlike in Tamil Nadu or Orissa [Odisha], NGOs did not play a major role" (Erramilli 2008: 84).

In contrast with Gujarat, Odisha's preparedness model reflects a state-driven approach with greater reliance on non-state partners. Development of the state disaster management agency was done with substantial input from the UNDP and local non-state actors were a focus of training initiatives (Odisha Government Official, March 28, 2014). Recounting interviews with Odisha state officials, Erramilli also noted that "respondents, by and large, repeated the official policy position that underscored the value of non-official participation. They appeared to have recognized the severe limitations of state abilities, which was evident in their cooptation of NGOs" (Erramilli 2008: 81).

The Andhra Pradesh government has also played a leading role in its preparedness efforts. At the same time, it has drawn on multiple academic partnerships, including inputs from the Central Research Institute for Dryland Agriculture (ICAR-CRIDA) for its drought forecasting efforts (Tejaswi and Kumar 2011: 447). There is less direct evidence of NGO activity in disaster preparedness efforts, and fewer preparedness activities in general than in Gujarat or Odisha. Nonetheless, what programs exist are clearly led by the state, in line with my expectations for a high-capacity state.

Finally, in Karnataka, one of the most successful preparedness initiatives has been implemented by an autonomous government body, the Karnataka State National Disaster Monitoring Centre (KSNDMC). This administrative setup allows the organization to hire specialized individuals from outside the traditional administrative hierarchy. The team is made up of scientists and support staff, rather than bureaucrats from Karnataka's lower-capacity administration (Chakrabarti 2019: 137). Thus, here there is an effort to draw from alternative non-state sources, academic rather than NGO, to build new disaster-specific capacity within the state. This is consistent with expectations for a state with lower levels of both government and NGO capacity.

Overall, these state cases reflect both the general tendency for Indian preparedness efforts to privilege state actors in developing and implementing programs with outside participation only where there are gaps in state capacity and available resources in the non-state arena.

4.2.2 State-Dominant Capacity

Similar to India, in case countries where the state has significant capacity relative to civil society, such as in Malawi and Zambia, I expect to see disaster preparedness efforts driven almost entirely by government, with little obvious presence of civil society participation.

Malawi is a useful example of a high-capacity state. Overall, interviews support the general perspective that bureaucratic capacity is relatively high in Malawi and particularly regarding levels of corruption, which are seen to be "vastly improved over many other African countries" (Bussell and Malcomb 2014: 155). This suggests the potential for a strong state role in disaster preparedness.

In practice, the development of disaster preparedness programs in Malawi has been tightly tied to the efforts of international donors and nongovernmental organizations. First, regarding donors, interviews highlighted that "Much of the recent efforts by donors have been concentrated on building capacity of Malawi's government to better respond to natural disasters, climate change, and other risk factors" (Bussell and Malcomb 2014: 115). Second, while the overall presence of domestic civil society organizations is relatively low, those that exist "are becoming increasingly connected and more influential in the stakeholder process on disaster planning" (Bussell and Malcomb 2014: 156). Thus, external groups have been actively working to support the government in its disaster preparedness efforts and "most government organizations appeared to be working with select donor organizations in an effective and cooperative manner that benefits vulnerable populations and results in increased invest- ment" (Bussell and Malcomb 2014: 156). This offers a nice illustration of the ways in which effective state capacity can be used to leverage even seemingly minimal non-state capacity to improve preparedness. While the government is a primary actor in preparedness efforts, rather than rely only on government institutions, Malawi's bureaucracy has engaged with civil society actors to enable them to play a more prominent role in Malawian preparedness efforts than otherwise expected, in concert with the government.

4.2.3 State-Led Capacity

Among the thirteen country cases, two exhibit high levels of both state and civil society capacity: Ghana and Senegal. I highlight here the approach taken in Ghana as an example of outcomes in this category.

Administratively, Ghana's national disasters-related body, NADMO, is pri- marily responsible for coordinating both state and nongovernmental actors in preparedness and response efforts, as expected by my argument. However, the effectiveness of NADMO is limited by its institutional development and rela- tive place in the government hierarchy. For example, "NADMO was unable to forecast and provide early warnings to affected areas so that stakeholders could prepare and respond to the emergency early. In addition, NADMO lacks an emergency operations center where all NGOs and stakeholders can meet and receive updated and accurate disaster assessments" (De Cuir et al. 2014: 70). Government policies on disaster preparedness and disaster risk reduction have also given a primary planning role to district authorities, rather than NADMO. "The district assemblies are the ultimate planning authorities and NADMO is not party to their deliberations or plans. Thus, the agency lacks the authority to force these assemblies to implement their DRR plans" (DeCuir et al 2014: 80–81).

Given these constraints, NADMO officials have leveraged their coordination role to push preparedness efforts. As one interviewee noted, "local civil society actors, in coordination with NADMO, have organized themselves into Disaster Volunteer Groups that focus on DRR and preparedness efforts through sustain- able farming and agricultural practices to combat potential natural disasters such as flooding. In addition, these groups are trained by NADMO officials on preparedness measures to reduce the effects felt when natural disasters occur" (DeCuir et al. 2014: 82). NADMO officials are also known to participate in training activities offered within civil society (DeCuir et al. 2014: 82).

In addition, civil society actors are pushing forward preparedness on their own. Smaller NGOs have become particularly active in this regard. "Rural Integrated Relief Services, for example, records natural disaster shocks, develops assessments of these shocks, educates individuals on issues concerning climate change, and offers training programs for disaster management. ABANTU for Development, another local NGO, raises awareness of gender issues in complex emergencies by bringing women into the mainstream of disaster prevention in Ghana" (DeCuir et al. 2014: 83). Large organizations are playing their own role, with "UNDP, United Nations Children's Fund (UNICEF), and other organizations ... pushing the preparedness agenda and helping NADMO and other government institutions to focus their efforts on these types of activities" (DeCuir et al. 2014: 81).

Ghana thus offers a model of state–society coordination in a country where national government policy has not effectively supported a fully state-led model. Decentralization of responsibilities to the district level makes it more difficult for a national-level body to coordinate state activities. Instead, NADMO relies on its ability to coordinate civil society actors to push forward the disaster preparedness agenda, while also allowing for outside efforts by other civil society actors.

4.2.4 Society-Reliant Capacity

Where the state has lower capacity, but civil society is relatively strong, I expect to see programs that are heavily reliant on the participation of these non-state actors. The countries falling into this category are the Gambia, Kenya, Mozambique, Togo, and Zimbabwe. In these contexts, a lack of internal state bureaucratic capacity leads the government to rely on non-state actors for the provision of even very basic public services (Brass 2012). This model may take multiple forms, depending on historical dynamics affecting the character of government institutions and the nature of civil society's strengths and weaknesses. Nonetheless, the anticipated result is a distribution of preparedness efforts that lies primarily within civil society organizations, not within the state.

Mozambique offers a particularly nice example for how such a capacity dynamic can lead to relatively successful preparedness outcomes in the context of a motivated state. Here, a state disaster management agency – the INGC – governs and directs all activities, of both government and civil society actors, across each country. This model may often involve collaboration in the planning of disaster preparedness programs, but the final say on what programs are implemented, how, and by whom, remains with the state, not with civil society actors.

The INGC plays the role of convener, having set up the CTGC (the disaster management technical council), which serves to guide all disaster preparedness and management activities. As a part of this, NGOs are incorporated into disaster management activities in multiple ways.

> One NGO representative noted that, "we have representatives from the disaster management department who go to the meetings that happen with the INGC, especially in times like now [during cyclone season] when they are worried about potential disasters and there are daily meetings, and they come back and then we have a meeting to decide on what to do . . . We work closely with the government in general." (Bussell and Malcomb 2014: 162)

As a result, the general sense among NGO representatives interviewed for this project was that disaster preparedness and response were both much better than they had been before the development of the INGC. As this NGO representative noted,

> NGOs have to be a part of the CTGC because the INGC is the coordinating body for all of the things that go on related to disasters and they need to know who is putting supplies where. They [the government] know all of the organizations acting in this area. In disasters, organizations can't act on their own. This makes the response much stronger. It is not like 2000 anymore, when it was really just chaos. (Bussell and Malcomb 2014: 162)

When there are specific preparedness programs that require activities on the ground in the periods between cyclone seasons, the government also leads the efforts to select and coordinate civil society actors to achieve these goals. This strategy serves to alleviate the capacity and human resources constraints of the government itself, by substituting NGO representatives for government employees in the field. "When an NGO starts working in Mozambique, they go to the government and tell them that they want to do work here and then the government helps allocate the NGO to areas of need. This is done through the Ministry of Foreign Affairs – they check with other ministries and look at the needs of the country and the skills of the NGO and then tell them where they can be of most use," noted the director of an international NGO operating in Mozambique (Bussell and Malcomb 2014: 162). What this looks like in practice, for example, is evident in the implementation of village disaster preparedness committees, which are used to train and mobilize leaders in rural communities:

> NGOs have been assigned particular areas of the country where they are in charge of working with local actors to train and implement committees.

> This is in part because neither the government nor any individual NGO has sufficient capacity to work in all regions of the country. But these organizations are also able to draw on their unique skills to facilitate development in capacity-constrained local environments. (Bussell and Malcomb 2014: 162)

Thus, this society-reliant model for disaster preparedness allows the Mozambique government to take advantage of civil society where it exists, particularly in areas where the state's own capacities may be lacking. While bureaucrats within the INGC have reasonable freedom from political involvement in their daily activities,

> the lack of trained bureaucrats in local areas does seem to limit preparedness and response in ways not directly related to politics. One observer noted that, "There are local level capacity gaps, but these are capacity gaps, not gaps in political will. DRR is still a relatively new field and there is not a lot of technical expertise available in DRR and DM." (Bussell & Malcomb 2014: 161)

4.2.5 Uncoordinated Capacity

In the final set of cases, Bangladesh, Ethiopia, and Pakistan, neither the government nor civil society has high levels of latent capacity upon which to draw for developing a disaster preparedness program. This is not to say that there will be no preparedness programs present, but where they do exist, I expect them again to reflect these similar (low) levels of capacity. I examine in greater detail an example of clearly uncoordinated activities in Bangladesh.

The dynamics of absence have clear implications in Bangladesh. Here, there is a centralized Ministry of Disaster Management and Relief that "also organizes the National Disaster Management Council that has representatives from the various institutions at national and local levels to tackle natural disasters in the country" (Shabhanaz and Bussell 2017: 16). In addition, "The National Disaster Management Regulatory Framework (NDMRF) provides a set of guidelines for disaster preparedness, risk reduction, and response." The framework was developed with the intent to mainstream risk reduction efforts within government, NGO, and private sector activities (Shabhanaz and Bussell 2017: 17).

However, this strategy does not effectively "account for government bodies outside of the traditional hierarchy of institutions. For example, almost all cyclone shelters in Bangladesh are primary schools built on raised ground, [which] effectively makes the shelters as much a budgetary concern for Ministry of Education as they are for Ministry of Disaster Management and

Relief" (Shabhanaz and Bussell 2017: 19). This has led to significant problems in disaster response, let alone preparedness, such as "when 48,000 families were displaced after Cyclone Aila, and spent over 14 months on the streets. This was because of lag time between constructing new houses, roads, and schools as each project falls under a different ministry in the government" (Shabhanaz and Bussell 2017: 20).

This lack of coordination extends to the government's relationship with civil society actors.

> In principle, the government, supported by the World Bank and Asian Development Bank, leads infrastructural projects, the UN leads development initiatives, and local NGOs take charge of voluntary efforts. In reality, though, the UN, given its history in assisting Bangladesh immediately after independence, plays an authoritative role in shaping disaster management policies with the central government. The government in turn, and as a result of being heavily politicized, fails to engage local elected public officials, NGOs, and civil society organizations in the process. The participation of NGOs and civil society organizations in policymaking has not been institutionalized. (Shabhanaz & Bussell 2017: 20)

Yet, as has been the case more generally since the aftermath of the 1974 drought (Hossain 2017), the "government relies on local NGOs, civil society organizations, and international agencies in building capacity of communities and providing emergency relief" (Shabhanaz & Bussell 2017: 25). This may take the form of relatively small NGOs – such as Muslim Aid – who "build capacity at the lowest level – in villages and urban wards – on cyclone and flood preparedness using locally sourced and trained volunteers" (Shabhanaz & Bussell 2017: 25). In contrast, substantially larger NGOs – such as BRAC – "provide disaster preparedness training through their numerous education programs and village-level meetings" (Shabhanaz & Bussell 2017: 25). In some cases, the government – via the Department of Disaster Management – has been able to partner with these larger organizations. This has resulted in "the development and implementation of several training modules to educate and prepare local communities against floods, cyclones and major natural disasters" (Shabhanaz & Bussell 2017: 25) Nonetheless, these efforts can only go so far given the limited resources available to state disaster staff at the local level.

These dynamics suggest that a lack of capacity in the government led Bangladesh to mobilize and organize its disaster-related activities insufficiently. Civil society actors themselves have mobilized related to natural disasters, but often after the fact, as a part of response efforts and in efforts to pressure the government to improve its disaster preparedness efforts (Shabhanaz and Bussell 2017: 32).

Table 20 Performance of theoretical expectations for country and Indian state capacity models

		State Capacity	
		Lower	**Higher**
	Lower	"Uncoordinated"	"State-Dominant"
		Bangladesh	**India**
		Ethiopia	**Malawi**
		Pakistan	**Zambia**
		Karnataka	**Gujarat**
Civil Society Capacity	**Higher**	"Society-Reliant"	"State-Led"
		Gambia	**Ghana**
		Kenya	**Senegal**
		Mozambique	**Andhra Pradesh**
		Togo	
		Zimbabwe	
		Odisha	

Note: Cases in bold match the expectations of my argument; those in italics display some variations from expectations.

4.3 Conclusion

Based on this discussion, there is substantial evidence to suggest that the character of disaster preparedness efforts reflects the latent capacity of state and non-state actors, as summarized in Table 20. As in Section 3, countries and states closely matching my expectations are shown in bold, while those displaying some variations from the expectations are highlighted in italics. Exceptions to my expectations tend to occur in places where civil society is expected to be more dominant, but these actors are constrained by broader restrictions on the independent activities of non-state actors. In the concluding section, I consider how the character of these approaches to disaster preparedness, combined with the political incentives described in Section 3, results in specific overall outcomes for disaster preparedness.

5 Assessing Outcomes and Conclusion

In this concluding section, I consider how well a combined consideration of political incentives and capacity helps us to understand disaster preparedness outcomes in the thirteen country case studies and Indian state cases. While the previous two sections looked specifically at the incentives of governments to engage in preparedness and the institutional shape of such programs, here I return to the overall outcomes relative to the international standards presented in Section 2 and ask whether my argument improves our ability to predict these outcomes in each case. I then consider the broader implications of this study for our understanding of government approaches to disaster preparedness and, more ambitiously, disaster risk reduction in the face of climate change.

5.1 Comparing Expectations to Outcomes

For this discussion, I organize the countries according to their expected disaster preparedness outcomes, based on the level of political incentives and character of overall capacity. These predicted outcomes are shown in Table 21. Countries and states shown in bold displayed disaster preparedness outcomes that strongly match the expectations of my argument. The countries in italics displayed preparedness performance that varied in certain ways from my expectations, but without a strong divergence. In no cases were outcomes significantly different from my expectations. I now consider the details of this assessment for each case.

5.1.1 Disaster Preparedness Performance in India

As in previous sections, I discuss India first, and it is the case that offers perhaps the best overall example of how political incentives combined with state capacity

Table 21 Match of theoretical expectations to empirical outcomes in disaster preparedness – country and Indian state cases

		Electoral Incentives	
		Lower	**Higher**
Capacity	**Lower**	"Minimal Performance"	"Substantial Effort"
		Gambia	**Bangladesh**
		Pakistan	**Ethiopia**
		Togo	*Kenya*
		Karnataka	**Mozambique**
			Zimbabwe
			Odisha
	Higher	"Window Dressing"	"Strong Performance"
		Ghana	**India**
		Senegal	**Malawi**
			Zambia
		Andhra Pradesh	
			Gujarat

Note: Countries in bold match the expectations of my argument; those in italics display some variations from expectations.

can produce strong outcomes. At the same time, I also draw attention to how the subnational cases reflect differing expectations and outcomes according to my argument.

Within India's states, there are clear variations in the relationship between electoral incentives, capacity, and preparedness outcomes. The strongest performer on preparedness overall is Gujarat, and the character of its performance is directly in line with the expectations of my argument. While Gujarat is also a relatively wealthy state, it did not invest substantially in preparedness policies until electoral conditions combined with repeated serious disasters to generate a political incentive to do so. Once this came to be, the state was able to move quickly and substantially toward a robust preparedness model due to significant internal bureaucratic capacity. In the context of relatively low civil society capacity, the state itself took charge of preparedness efforts and has been recognized for the substantial reductions in human and capital losses these improvements have produced during recent hazards (Rawat 2019).

Odisha is a lower-capacity state, but in a context where electoral incentives and leveraging of civil society could potentially result in considerable efforts to prepare. This is precisely the observed outcome, as a devastating cyclone combined with a highly competitive electoral environment to motivate the state government toward a radically different model for disaster preparedness. In implementing this model, however, the state has faced limitations due to somewhat lower levels of state capacity than in the cases of Andhra Pradesh and Gujarat.

In Andhra Pradesh, the state seems poised to engage in substantial efforts to prepare for natural disasters, particularly given its high levels of state capacity, but has underperformed relative to states such as Gujarat and Odisha. While the state introduced a disaster management authority in line with national policy and has made progress in areas such as risk assessment and monitoring, it has not made preparedness a political priority in the same way as some other states. This is in line with the expectations of my argument for a state that has lower electoral incentives to prepare. It has engaged in the minimum activities that increase basic preparedness, but not in ways that dramatically reduce the risk of disasters in the state.

Karnataka displays the lowest preparedness of the Indian cases considered in detail here. While it has implemented programs in a few areas, such as hazard monitoring, the overall preparedness model is uneven and lacks considerable government attention. This is consistent with my expectations in a state that faces minimal electoral incentives to invest in preparedness and is not equipped with substantial state or civil society capacity to mobilize preparedness efforts otherwise.

In India as a whole, there is a substantial central government effort to invest in institutions of preparedness, intended to support state efforts. Yet, despite high levels of wealth relative to the other country cases, these efforts did not emerge in a comprehensive manner until a substantial disaster, in the form of the 2004 tsunami, imposed significant damages across multiple electorally important states. It was only then that the central government began to leverage its substantial bureaucratic capacity to develop resources that could not only assist in hazard response, but also supply the policy guidelines and training needed for states to improve their performance. This resulted in an overall strong model for disaster preparedness that, while not without areas for improvement, provides a substantial foundation for minimizing disaster risk, even in the absence of substantial participation from civil society actors.

5.1.2 Anticipated Strong Performance

I continue the evaluation with the other countries exhibiting both high levels of electoral incentives and high capacity, where I would expect to see the strongest performance on disaster preparedness. These countries are Malawi and Zambia, in addition to India.

In Malawi, outcomes are in line with my expectations. The country does well on the disaster preparedness measures overall but is still somewhat limited in its performance relative to places like India. While it was difficult to assess political incentives in this case, the high capacity of state actors, combined with a small number of highly active donor agencies and NGOs, has allowed the state to push forward on its preparedness efforts in a substantial way.

For Zambia, we see medium level performance on the components of disaster preparedness. The state clearly coordinates disaster preparedness activities by both the bureaucracy and civil society actors and these efforts are directly motivated by past exposure to natural hazards. At the same time, there is little evidence that politicians themselves take seriously disaster preparedness as a core element of their political agenda. In this context, I would expect performance on preparedness and related efforts to continue to improve alongside increased electoral competition.

5.1.3 Anticipated Substantial Effort

In a second set of cases, Bangladesh, Ethiopia, Kenya, Mozambique, and Zimbabwe, my argument anticipates medium levels of disaster preparedness, which reflect political incentives to prepare crossed with limitations from lower levels of capacity, often within the state. Thus, there should be efforts to invest in preparedness, even if the goals of these efforts are difficult to meet in the context of lower capacity.

Bangladesh exhibits strong political incentives to invest in preparedness and these dynamics are clearly evident in overall preparedness programming. Interestingly, the degree to which Bangladesh outperforms my expectations seems to be due to the role of civil society actors, despite limitations on the state's ability to coordinate these activities effectively. Here, it is worth noting that my overall strategy for measuring non-state capacity may not fully account for the predominance of natural hazard-related civil society activity, relative to other non-state actors. Thus, there is a more substantial level of preparedness programming than anticipated. The risk over time, however, is that if the government is unable to coordinate ongoing activities effectively, there may be considerable duplication of effort and confusion in response at the time of hazard events.

In Ethiopia, preparedness efforts reflect political incentives combined with an empowered, if lower capacity, bureaucracy. The long history of past exposure in this case means that politicians are well-acquainted with the risks of natural hazards. These state actors have enabled a disaster management body to design and implement its programs and given it the power to coordinate efforts with civil society actors in a highly structured manner. Thus, while there are still gaps in Ethiopia's overall preparedness profile, the country has displayed considerable effort to overcome limitations to capacity both inside and outside the state, enabling it to achieve relatively strong preparedness outcomes.

Mozambique also demonstrates the relatively long-term effects of high impact disasters. High intensity cyclones in Mozambique have increased the political salience of natural hazards for Mozambique's politicians, motivating investments in preparedness even multiple years after these events. As in Ethiopia, Mozambique has a highly empowered disaster management body with the purview to coordinate activities with civil society actors. The effect of substantial natural hazards has been to incentivize politicians to support development of a strong disaster management agency, again serving to demonstrate an increase in disaster-specific capacity within the state. This body is then able to mobilize civil society actors in ways that increase overall capacity. There are still issues in the Mozambiquan model, but the outcomes observed here are largely consistent with an argument that emphasizes the importance of political incentives and capacity in generating substantial efforts to increase preparedness.

Kenya, in contrast, somewhat under performs my expectations, due in large part to the lack of significant direct government efforts toward disaster preparedness. Voter interest in issues other than past exposure has affected the perceptions of politicians that disaster preparedness can be used to build political advantage in Kenya's competitive electoral environment. In addition, the low levels of state capacity in Kenya mean that there is little opportunity for internal program development without substantial political interest. As a result, the efforts that do exist are left largely to civil society, which is limited in its capacity to pursue the range of initiatives laid out in standards for disaster preparedness.

The final case in this category is Zimbabwe. Here, there are some preparedness initiatives in place, but the state is limited in its capacity and places its own constraints on the activities of civil society, in ways that curb more substantial progress. This means that even while there are long-term incentives to invest due to past exposure, capacity is so limited as to place barriers on any major political efforts. While I would expect to see more effort in this case, these outcomes are generally consistent with the argument.

5.1.4 Anticipated "Window Dressing"

In two countries, Ghana and Senegal, the alignment of political incentives and capacity is such that I expect to see some evidence of disaster preparedness efforts, but in ways that reflect limited political incentives to prepare. In other words, these are states that have the capacity to prepare, but lack the political incentive to do so.

For Ghana, the overall outcomes are in line with the predictions of my argument. A disaster management agency was put in place, but it was situated institutionally in a manner that gives it limited authority to act relative to other government institutions. State bureaucrats demonstrate their capacity to coordinate with civil society actors to push forward preparedness efforts but must act within the constraints of the national disaster management agency's placement within the government. And, whereas politicians are acting in a competitive electoral environment, the general lack of exposure within the population limits citizen support for preparedness efforts. Thus, there is a medium level of performance that is in line with more limited electoral incentives in a higher-capacity state.

In the Senegalese case, there is substantial activity in disaster preparedness by state actors, but these actions are spread across a variety of politicized agencies and not well coordinated. This reflects a lack of overall electoral incentives to coordinate government actors within a preparedness program. There are also many preparedness efforts among civil society actors, but again, without coordination by a central agency that could ensure combined benefits of this work and minimize risks of duplicative effort. As a result, while preparedness activities are clearly visible, their character reflects my expectations in that they lack the political oversight and organization that could lead to substantial preparedness.

5.1.5 Anticipated Low Performance

The remaining country cases – the Gambia, Pakistan, and Togo – exhibit levels of electoral incentives and capacity suggesting relatively low outcomes on preparedness.

The Gambia's overall performance on preparedness is in line with my theoretical expectations. Low levels of past exposure in the population and constraints on the opposition limit political incentives to prepare. Even so, the government has implemented a viable disaster management body with the potential to push forward preparedness initiatives. Where these efforts fail is in the government's lack of coordination, and even competition, with civil society actors in the preparedness space. While civil society actors have relatively higher capacity in Gambia than the state, the government's failure to coordinate has resulted in substantially limited progress on preparedness.

Pakistan's disaster preparedness performance is somewhat better than I would expect, but the character of these efforts is in line with the expectations of my argument. Political actors face electoral concerns but are not highly motivated by past exposure. In addition, complicated institutional dynamics related to authority over disaster preparedness programming mean that national, more than local, politicians can claim credit for preparedness outcomes. As a result, preparedness initiatives are primarily the purview of local bureaucrats who are highly resource constrained. Thus, much of what is observed in practice are high-level program initiatives with variable implementation at the local level.

For Togo, disaster preparedness is minimal, at best. In this case, it seems that even where there was some knowledge of needs for general disaster preparedness, the lack of substantial past exposure to direct these efforts and lack of funds to support general development, let alone preparedness efforts, stymied whatever motivations existed for developing a preparedness agenda. This is a clear example where the combination of limited electoral incentives and limited capacity results in highly limited preparedness outcomes.

Overall, with some interesting nuances, this discussion suggests that the argument laid out in this volume performs remarkably well in predicting three core dynamics of disaster preparedness: the character of elite motivation for preparedness, the governance of preparedness initiatives, and overall levels of success in achieving preparedness, as measured by international standards. At a minimum, this argument provides a substantially stronger explanation for these outcomes than those laid out in previous research.

5.2 Implications and Conclusion

What does this argument imply for how to approach evaluations of disaster preparedness in other contexts and, perhaps most importantly, ongoing and future work in broader areas of disaster risk reduction and climate change?

5.2.1 Generalizability

The case studies evaluated here constitute a significant portion of countries in Africa and South Asia. As noted in Section 1, I expect the argument to hold in many other countries in these regions and, quite plausibly, other areas of the Global South. In addition, the dynamics of political incentives and capacity are likely to be just as relevant in the Global North, where much research on natural hazards has focused. In these countries, generally higher levels of capacity should mean that the dominant factor is political incentives, as highlighted in existing work. What must be considered to understand preparedness, then, is whether past exposure and electoral competition generate conditions in which previously exposed voters play a dominant role in political decision-making. This is likely to become even more relevant as shifts in climate conditions result in changing patterns of hazards around the world.

5.2.2 Disaster Preparedness and Climate Change

The hydro-meteorological character of the primary hazards considered in this study is particularly important when evaluating how to apply these lessons to our expectations about climate change-related hazards. I earlier provided evidence that natural hazards are increasing in their frequency globally and this is occurring alongside, and is plausibly related to, changes in global air and water temperatures. This suggests not only that there will be more hazards, but that they are likely to occur with differing intensities and in different places than in the past. What does this mean for how governments are likely to respond to such hazards in the future?

One possible descriptive outcome would be the merging of government efforts to prepare for, and reduce the risks of, disasters with climate change-related initiatives. Over the course of this study, it became clear that governments were beginning to consider links between disaster-related programming and climate change adaptation, for both substantive and financial reasons. While in some cases this led to difficulties with coordination across departments, the general sense was that a unified approach could maximize overall resources, particularly around risk reduction.

Yet, which countries should be successful in these types of coordinated efforts? I anticipate that whether countries can move forward on a climate change-informed natural hazards policy agenda depends on quite similar factors to those considered here. Political elites will evaluate the relative implications of climate adaptations and the strength of their political position. The factors that affect these dynamics may differ from those central to disaster preparedness, however, given significant and often more visible investments associated with strategies such as decarbonization (Guy ND).

In practice, this could also mean that countries with the capacity to prepare for hazards – states with stronger internal bureaucracies – may lag in their responsiveness due to a lack of prior exposure. For example, countries with moderate average temperatures, for which small changes do not have as drastic of consequences as in higher average temperature countries, may fail to address the risks of these temperature changes despite having the capacity to do so. These political actors are only likely to engage in significant efforts when the threats of these changes become obvious to the voting population through direct exposure to a hazard. As a result, it may require experience with significant new climate-induced hazard events to motivate political actors to prepare appropriately.

In contrast, governments in areas with a history of past exposure, where hazards may change but are unlikely to disappear, could be better poised to prepare for such events than might be expected based on economic resources. External actors with an interest in supporting climate change adaptation could benefit from approaching these policy actors from the perspective of reducing risks with which governments are already familiar, rather than developing entirely new frameworks for fundamentally related policy areas. This would enable motivated actors to act, by providing additional resources and external capacity to effectively compliment ongoing internal efforts.

Overall, these dynamics suggest that substantial climate change adaptation, and the implications of these policies for natural disaster risks, is not necessarily going to appear in the richest countries first. Countries facing repeated, and potentially worsening, threats from climate-induced hazards may instead be at the forefront of techniques and strategies to reduce these risks. Yet, these countries will not all have the capacity to implement substantial programs and they may also face increased risks due to failures of richer nations to invest in climate change-minimizing reforms. Our global interest may then be best served by efforts to support risk-reducing climate change adaptation in the Global South. Insights and innovations from these efforts can then be leveraged to inform policies in the Global North as political incentives inevitably evolve in the wake of changing hazard profiles.

References

Agnihotri, Anustubh, Zachary Child, Anna Koob, and Rachel Wald. 2014. "Flooding in Senegal and the Gambia: Current Challenges and the Future of Disaster Risk Management," in Jennifer Bussell, Ed. *Institutional Capacity for Natural Disasters: Case Studies in Africa*. Climate Change and African Political Stability Program Student Working Paper No. 6., pp. 26–65.

Aldrich, Daniel. 2010. "Separate and Unequal: Post-Tsunami Aid Distribution in Southern India," *Social Science Quarterly*, 91(4): 1369–1389.

Aldrich, Daniel P. 2012. *Building Resilience: Social Capital in Post-Disaster Recovery*. Chicago: The University of Chicago Press.

Bahadur, Aditya, Emma Lovell, and Florence Pichon. 2016. "Strengthening Disaster Management in India: A Review of Five State Disaster Management Plans," London, ODI.

Baker, Justin, Matthew Guevara, Christian Peratsakis, and Milad Pournik. 2014. "Diversity of National Response: Zimbabwe and Zambia," in Jennifer Bussell, Ed. *Institutional Capacity for Natural Disasters: Case Studies in Africa*. Climate Change and African Political Stability Program Student Working Paper No. 6., pp. 166–205.

Bechtel, Michael M. and Jens Hainmueller. 2011. "How Lasting is Voter Gratitude? An Analysis of the Short- and Long-Term Electoral Returns to Beneficial Policy," *American Journal of Political Science*, 55(4): 851–867.

Bhavnani, Rikhil R. and Bethany Lacina. 2015. "The Effects of Weather-Induced Migration on Sons of the Soil Riots in India," *World Politics*, 67 (4): 760–794.

Bolhken, Anjali Thomas. 2013. *Democratization from Above: The Logic of Local Democracy in the Developing World*. Cambridge, UK: Cambridge University Press.

Brass, Jennifer. 2012. "Blurring Boundaries: The integration of NGOs into Governance in Kenya," *Governance*, 25: 209–235.

Brass, Jennifer. 2016. *Allies or Adversaries: NGOs and the State in Africa*. New York: Cambridge University Press.

Bussell, Jennifer. 2012. *Corruption and Reform in India: Public Services in the Digital Age*. New York: Cambridge University Press.

Bussell, Jennifer. Ed. 2014. Institutional Capacity for Natural Disasters: Case Studies in Africa. Climate Change and African Political Stability Program Student Working Paper No. 6.

Bussell, Jennifer. 2017. "Politicizing Preparation: Evidence from India on the Incentives for Disaster Preparedness." CEPSA Research Brief, Austin: Robert S. Strauss Center for International Security and Law.

Bussell, Jennifer 2019. *Clients and Constituents: Political Responsiveness in Patronage Democracies*. Modern South Asia Series, Oxford: Oxford University Press.

Bussell, Jennifer and Adam Colligan. 2014. "Introduction," in Jennifer Bussell, Ed. *Institutional Capacity for Natural Disasters: Case Studies in Africa*. Climate Change and African Political Stability Program Student Working Paper No. 6., pp. 1–25.

Bussell, Jennifer and Dylan Malcomb. 2014. "Natural Disasters in Malawi and Mozambique: Capacity and Cooperation," in Jennifer Bussell, Ed. *Institutional Capacity for Natural Disasters: Case Studies in Africa*. Climate Change and African Political Stability Program Student Working Paper No. 6., pp. 134–165.

Bussell, Jennifer and Asim Fayaz. 2017. "The Political Economy of Disaster Preparedness and Risk Reduction in Pakistan," CEPSA Research Brief No. 5. Austin: Robert S. Strauss Center for International Security and Law.

Cammett, Melanie and Lauren M. MacLean. 2011. "Introduction: The Political Consequences of Non-State Social Welfare in the Global South," *Studies in Comparative International Development*, 46(1): 1–21.

Cammett, Melanie and Lauren M. MacLean, Eds. 2014. *The Politics of Non-State Social Welfare*. Ithaca, NY: Cornell University Press.

Centeno, Miguel A., Atul Kohli, and Deborah J. Yashar. 2017. *States in the Developing World*. Cambridge: Cambridge University Press.

Chakrabarti, P. G. Dhar. 2019. *Disaster Risk and Resilience in India: An Analytic Study*. Delhi: Ministry of Home Affairs, Government of India.

Chhibber, Pradeep and Irfan Nooruddin. 2004. "Do Party Systems Count? The Number of Parties and Government Performance in the Indian States," *Comparative Political Studies*, 37: 152–187.

Cho, Seok-Ju. 2009. "Retrospective Voting and Political Representation," *American Journal of Political Science*, 53(2): 276–291.

Cohen, Charles and Eric Werker. 2008. "The Political Economy of 'Natural' Disasters," *Journal of Conflict Resolution*, 52(6): 795–819.

Cole, Shawn, Andrew Healy, and Eric Werker. 2012. "Do Voters Demand Responsive Governments? Evidence from Indian Disaster Relief," *Journal of Development Economics* 97(2): 167–181.

Collier, David and Steven Levitsky. 1997. "Democracy with Adjectives: Conceptual Innovation in Comparative Research," *World Politics*, 49: 43–51.

DeCuir, Sarah, Rachel Fuerst, Christina Iannuzzi, and Jaclyn Leaver. 2014. "Donors, Disasters, and Development: Flooding in Ghana and Togo," in Jennifer Bussell, Ed. *Institutional Capacity for Natural Disasters: Case Studies in Africa*. Climate Change and African Political Stability Program Student Working Paper No. 6., pp. 66–94.

Erramilli, Bala Prasad. 2008. Disaster Management in India: Analysis of Factors Affecting Capacity Building. *Political Science Dissertations*, Georgia State University. Paper 15.

Evans, Peter and James E. Rauch. 1999. "Bureaucracy and Growth: A Cross-National Analysis of the Effects of "Weberian" State Structures on Economic Growth," *American Sociological Review*, 64(5): 748–765.

Fox, Justin and Richard Van Weelden. 2015. "Hoping for the Best, Unprepared for the Worst," *Journal of Public Economics*, 130: 59–65.

Gailmard, Sean and John W. Patty. 2019. "Preventing Prevention," *American Journal of Political Science*, 63(2): 342–352.

Geddes, Barbara, Joseph Wright, and Erica Frantz. 1994. *How Dictatorships Work*. Cambridge, UK: Cambridge University Press.

Geddes, Barbara, Joseph Wright, and Erica Frantz. 2014. "Autocratic Breakdown and Regime Transitions: A New Data Set," *Perspectives on Politics*, 12(2): 313–331.

Gottipati, Sruthi, 2013. "Mass evacuation saves lives as cyclone leaves trail of destruction," October 13, Reuters, www.reuters.com/article/india-cyclone-phailin-odisha-andhra-idINDEE99C00C20131013, Accessed December 28, 2022

Gulzar, Saad and Benjamin J. Pasquale. 2015, "Politicians, Bureaucrats, and Development: Evidence from India," *American Political Science Review*, 111 (1): 162–183.

Guy, Johnathan. No Date. "Comparative Cleavage Formation in Climate Politics: Bargaining, State Capacity, and Industrial Structures." Working Paper.

Habyarimana, James, Macartan Humphreys, Daniel Posner, and Jeremy Weinstein. 2007. "Why Does Ethnic Diversity Undermine Public Goods Provision?" *American Political Science Review*, 101(4): 709–725.

Harriman, Lindsey. 2013. "Cyclone Phaillin in India: Early Warning and Timely Actions Saved Lives," United Nations Environment Program. https://na.unep.net/geas/getUNEPPageWithArticleIDScript.php?article_id=106, Accessed October 23, 2023.

Hassan, Mai. 2020. *Regime Threats and State Solutions: Bureaucratic Loyalty and Embeddedness in Kenya*. Cambridge Studies in Comparative Politics. New York: Cambridge University Press.

Healy, Andrew and Neil Malhotra. 2009. "Myopic Voters and Natural Disaster Policy," *American Political Science Review*, 103(3): 387–406.

Hindu, The. 2022. "Ready for the worst: on government's better preparedness for cyclones," December 13. www.thehindu.com/opinion/editorial/ready-for-the-worst-on-governments-better-preparedness-for-cyclones/article66254900.ece, Accessed December 28, 2022.

Hossain, Naomi. 2017. *The Aid Lab: Understanding Bangladesh's Unexpected Success*. Oxford: Oxford University Press.

Hsiang, Solomon M. and Amir S. Jina. 2014. "The Causal Effect of Environmental Catastrophe on Long-Run Economic Growth: Evidence from 6,700 Cyclones," NBER Working Paper 20352, July.

Hsiang, Solomon M., Marsahll Burke, and Edward Miguel. 2013. "Quantifying the Influence of Climate on Human Conflict," *Science*, 341(6151): 1235367.

Hsiang, Solomon M. and Daiju Narita. 2012. "Adaptation to Cyclone Risk: Evidence from the Global Cross-Section," *Climate Change Economics*, 3(2): 1250011, 1–28.

Institute for Economics & Peace. 2020. *Ecological Threat Register 2020: Understanding Ecological Threats, Resilience and Peace*. Sydney: IEP. www.visionofhumanity.org/wp-content/uploads/2020/10/ETR_2020_web-1.pdf.

Keefer, Philip. 2009. "Disastrous Consequences: The Political Economy of Disaster Risk Reduction," Paper commissioned by the Joint World Bank – United Nations Project on the Economics of Disaster Relief.

Keefer, Philip, Eric Neumayer, and Thomas Plumper. 2011. "Earthquake Propensity and the Politics of Mortality Prevention," *World Development*, 39(9): 1530–1541.

Khemani, Stuti. 2003. "Partisan politics and intergovernmental transfers in India," Policy Research Working Paper Series 3016, The World Bank.

Levitsky, Steven and María Victoria Murillo. 2009. "Variation in Institutional Strength," *Annual Review of Political Science*, 12: 115–133.

MacLean, Lauren M., Jennifer N. Brass, Sanya Carley, Ashraf El-Arini and Scott Breen. 2015. "Democracy and the Distribution of NGOs Promoting Renewable Energy in Africa," *The Journal of Development Studies*, 51(6): 725–742. https://doi.org/10.1080/00220388.2014.989994.

Martin, Max. 2007. "Farce Follows Disaster," *India Together*. https://indiatogether.org/disaster-relief.

Ministry of Home Affairs. 2013. "Report of the Task Force: A Review of the Disaster Management Act," 2005. New Delhi, Government of India.

Mohanty, Debabrata. 2021. "How Odisha's Model of Disaster Preparedness Came into Being," Hindustan Times, May 26. https://www.hindustantimes.com/cities/cyclone-yaas-how-odisha-s-model-of-disaster-preparedness-came-into-being-101621969683964.html.

National Centre for Disaster Management. 2002. *The Report of the High Powered Committee on Disaster Management*. New Delhi: Indian Institute of Disaster Management.

National Disaster Management Agency. 2008. *National Disaster Management Guidelines: Management of Cyclones*. New Delhi, India: Government of India.

O'Reilly, Colin and Ryan H. Murphy. 2022. "An Index Measuring State Capacity, 1789-2018," *Economica*, 89: 713–745.

Panda, Prasant Kumar. 2016. "Economic and Political Determinants of Central Fiscal Transfer in India: A Dynamic Panel Analysis of State Level Data," *The Journal of Developing Areas*, 50(2): 329–347, Spring.

Rawat, Mukesh. 2019. "Cyclone Vayu spares Gujarat: 1 n 1998, a cyclone rained death, killed thousands in state," India Today, June 13. www.indiato day.in/india/story/cyclone-vayu-gujarat-landfall-1998-kandla-destruction-1548051-2019-06-13, Accessed October 6, 2023.

Ray-Bennett, Nibedita. 2016. "Learning from Deaths in Disasters," *Middle East Journal* (online).

Reimer, Loren, Tiffany Tripson, Savin Ven Johnson, and Wes Ven Johnson. 2014. "Divergent Roles for the State: Disaster Management in Ethiopia and Kenya," in Jennifer Bussell, Ed. *Institutional Capacity for Natural Disasters: Case Studies in Africa*. Climate Change and African Political Stability Program Student Working Paper No. 6, pp. 95–133.

Rothstein, Bo and Teorell, Jan. 2008. "What Is Quality of Government? A Theory of Impartial Government Institutions," *Governance*, 21: 165–190. https://doi.org/10.1111/j.1468-0491.2008.00391.x.

Sarma, G.V.V. 2015. "India: National Progress on the Implementation of the Hyogo Framework for Action (2013-2015)," National HFA Monitor report, PreventionWeb, http://www.preventionweb.net/english/hyogo/progress/reports/.

Shabhanaz, Rashid Diya and Jennifer Bussell. 2017. "Disaster Preparedness in Bangladesh," CEPSA Research Brief No. 7. Austin: Robert S. Strauss Center for International Security and Law (co-authored with).

Self, Darin. 2020. "Survival Through Strength: How Strong Party Organizations Help Authoritarian Regimes Survive," Working Paper. www.darinself.com/assets/files/survival.pdf Accessed December 29, 2022.

Singh, Rajendra. 2023. "Cyclone Biparjoy: How Efficient Early Warning System Minimized Loss of Lives, Damages," The Times of India, June 20, www.indiatoday.in/opinion-columns/story/cyclone-biparjoy-how-efficient-early-warning-system-minimised-loss-of-lives-damage-opinion-2395307-2023-06-20, Accessed October 13, 2023.

Stroup, Sarah. 2012. *Borders Among Activists: International NGOs in the United States, Britain, and France*. Ithaca: Cornell University Press.

Tejaswi, Lakshmi and Ramacharla Pradeep Kumar. 2011. "Disaster mitigation and management for Andhra Pradesh: An appraisal," *International Journal of Earth Sciences and Engineering*, 4(3): 443-453.

World Bank Sustainable Development Department. 2009. "Making Development Climate Resilient: A World Bank Strategy for Sub-Saharan Africa," World Bank Report No. 46947-AFR. Washington, DC: World Bank.

World Bank and United Nations. 2010. *Natural Hazards, UnNatural Disasters: The Economics of Effective Prevention*. Washington, DC: World Bank.

Interviews

Odisha State Government Official #1, March 26, 2014
National Institute of Disaster Management (India) Official, March 24, 2014
National Disaster Management Authority (India) Official, March 25, 2014
Odisha State Government Official #2, March 26, 2014

Acknowledgments

I thank all of the individuals involved in the CCAPS and CEPSA MINERVA initiatives, especially Josh Busby, Ashley Moran, and Kate Weaver, and all of the students who worked on parts of this project – Anustubh Agnihotri, Justin Baker, Adam Colligan, Sarah DeCuir, Sabhanaz Rashid Diya, Asim Fayaz, Rachel Fuerst, Matthew Guevara, Christina Iannuzzi, Anna Koob, Jaclyn Leaver, Dylan Malcomb, Christian Peratsakis, Milad Pournik, Loren Reimer, Tiffany Tripson, Savin Ven Johnson, Wes Ven Johnson, and Rachel Wald. I am also grateful to Rachel Brulé, Thad Dunning, Johnathan Guy, Mai Hassan, Jessica Rich, and the series editors, Ben Ross Schneider, Rachel Beatty Riedl, and Maya Tudor, as well as two anonymous reviewers, for their generous and insightful inputs, feedback, and support for this project.

Cambridge Elements ≡

Politics of Development

Rachel Beatty Riedl
Einaudi Center for International Studies and Cornell University

Rachel Beatty Riedl is the Director and John S. Knight Professor of the Einaudi Center for International Studies and Professor in the Government Department and School of Public Policy at Cornell University. Riedl is the author of the award-winning *Authoritarian Origins of Democratic Party Systems in Africa* (2014) and co-author of *From Pews to Politics: Religious Sermons and Political Participation in Africa* (with Gwyneth McClendon, 2019). She studies democracy and institutions, governance, authoritarian regime legacies, and religion and politics in Africa. She serves on the Editorial Committee of World Politics and the Editorial Board of African Affairs, Comparative Political Studies, Journal of Democracy, and Africa Spectrum. She is co-host of the podcast Ufahamu Africa.

Ben Ross Schneider
Massachusetts Institute of Technology

Ben Ross Schneider is Ford International Professor of Political Science at MIT and Director of the MIT-Brazil program. Prior to moving to MIT in 2008, he taught at Princeton University and Northwestern University. His books include *Business Politics and the State in 20th Century Latin America* (2004), *Hierarchical Capitalism in Latin America* (2013), *Designing Industrial Policy in Latin America: Business-Government Relations and the New Developmentalism* (2015), and *New Order and Progress: Democracy and Development in Brazil* (2016). He has also written on topics such as economic reform, democratization, education, labor markets, inequality, and business groups.

Maya Tudor
Oxford University

Maya Tudor is Professor of Politics and Public Policy, Blavatnik School of Government and Fellow, St. Hilda's College, at Oxford University. She researches democracy and nationalism in the developing world, with a focus on South Asia, and is the author of two books, Promise of Power and Varieties of Nationalism.

Advisory Board

Yuen Yuen Ang, *University of Michigan*
Catherine Boone, *London School of Economics*
Melani Cammett, *Harvard University* (former editor)
Stephan Haggard, *University of California, San Diego*
Prerna Singh, *Brown University*
Dan Slater, *University of Michigan*

About the Series

The Element series *Politics of Development* provides important contributions on both established and new topics on the politics and political economy of developing countries. A particular priority is to give increased visibility to a dynamic and growing body of social science research that examines the political and social determinants of economic development, as well as the effects of different development models on political and social outcomes.

Cambridge Elements ≡

Politics of Development

Elements in the Series

A full series listing is available at: www.cambridge.org/EPOD

www.ingramcontent.com/pod-product-compliance
Ingram Content Group UK Ltd.
Pitfield, Milton Keynes, MK11 3LW, UK
UKHW020820300125
454392UK00011B/456